T0333389

"This guidebook is innovative as it helps autistic young people own their autism diagnosis, whereas it's likely the pathway thus far has been directed by a medical and/or parental perspective. This book assists adults to support autistic young people to find a safe space to explore their autistic identity, diagnosis and newfound life trajectory." – **Carly Jones** MBE, British Autism Advocate

"*Autism, Identity and Me* not only reflects Rebecca's ethos, it is a structured, easy to follow, informative and invaluable text which covers all areas of autism from what it actually is through to every element of the day to day life of an autistic child. I will be using this book in my own practice." – **Andrew Whitehouse**, SEND Consultant, Andrew Whitehouse Ltd

"Feeling different can be an upsetting, frustrating and terrifying experience, especially as a child. Rebecca's book is a great resource to help young people and the adults supporting them to navigate an autism diagnosis." – **Dr Jenna Kenyani**, Equality, Diversity, Inclusion and Wellbeing Adviser, University of Liverpool

"Rebecca's book is a great resource for guiding strength-based conversations about a young person's autistic identity. The book focuses on individual similarities and differences, whilst encouraging a sense of shared identity and connection to others. This is a great resource for supporting young people to explore their individual strengths and skills, whilst developing a sense of pride. A recommended read!" – **Dr Claire Prosser** BEM, Educational Psychologist, Spectropolis – Pay it Forward

"This book has helped me get a grip on my autism and understand it more. It allows me to see the reasons, know why I'm doing all this stuff that neurotypicals wouldn't do, and makes me feel better – good – that I wasn't alone in this." – **Daniel**, Young Person

ACCESS YOUR ONLINE RESOURCES

Autism, Identity and Me: A Professional and Parent Guide to Support a Positive Understanding of Autistic Identity is accompanied by a number of printable online materials, designed to ensure this resource best supports your professional needs.

Activate your online resources:

Go to https://resourcecentre.routledge.com/speechmark and click on the cover of this book.

Click the 'Sign in' or 'Request access' button and follow the instructions in order to access the resources.

AUTISM, IDENTITY AND ME

This informative and engaging guidebook provides key adults – parents, school staff and therapists – with the tools needed to support children and young people as they develop a positive understanding of their autistic identity.

The guidebook is designed to accompany the *Autism, Identity and Me* workbook, building the adult's understanding of autism and autistic identity, expanding upon the themes introduced, and offering a clear and structured programme of sessions to guide the young person through the workbook. Content has been shaped by autistic advisors and contributors, with first-hand experiences woven throughout, alongside examples of 'possible prompts', what to focus on as a lead adult, and a variety of concrete, neurodiversity-affirming strategies.

Having a positive understanding of your autistic identity is an indicator of higher self-esteem and wellbeing as an adult. This guidebook supports the development of this and will be valuable for all adults working with autistic children and young people aged 10+.

Rebecca Duffus BSc, PGCE, MA is an experienced Advisory Teacher with a Psychology Degree and a Masters in Autism and Education. She has many years of experience working with students and educators in both mainstream and specialist education settings as well as within local authority and education services. Rebecca has been a speaker at conferences across the UK, developed a range of parent programmes, and provides training and coaching for settings. Rebecca is passionate about celebrating neurodiversity.

AUTISM, IDENTITY AND ME

A PROFESSIONAL AND PARENT GUIDE TO SUPPORT A POSITIVE UNDERSTANDING OF AUTISTIC IDENTITY

Rebecca Duffus

Illustrations by Beth Smith and Rebecca Duffus

Routledge
Taylor & Francis Group

LONDON AND NEW YORK

Designed cover image: © Lisa Dynan

First published 2023
by Routledge
4 Park Square, Milton Park, Abingdon, Oxon OX14 4RN

and by Routledge
605 Third Avenue, New York, NY 10158

Routledge is an imprint of the Taylor & Francis Group, an informa business

© 2023 Rebecca Duffus

The right of Rebecca Duffus to be identified as author of this work has been asserted in accordance with sections 77 and 78 of the Copyright, Designs and Patents Act 1988.

All rights reserved. The purchase of this copyright material confers the right on the purchasing institution to photocopy or download pages which bear the companion website icon or a copyright line at the bottom of the page. No other parts of this book may be reprinted or reproduced or utilised in any form or by any electronic, mechanical, or other means, now known or hereafter invented, including photocopying and recording, or in any information storage or retrieval system, without permission in writing from the publishers.

Trademark notice: Product or corporate names may be trademarks or registered trademarks, and are used only for identification and explanation without intent to infringe.

British Library Cataloguing-in-Publication Data
A catalogue record for this book is available from the British Library

Library of Congress Cataloging-in-Publication Data
Names: Duffus, Rebecca, 1986- author. | Smith, Beth (Illustrator), illustrator
Title: Autism, identity and me : a professional and parent guide to support a positive understanding of autistic identity / Rebecca Duffus ; illustrations by Beth Smith and Rebecca Duffus.
Description: 1. | Abingdon, Oxon ; New York, NY : Routledge, 2023. | Includes bibliographical references and index. | Summary -- Provided by publisher.
Identifiers: LCCN 2022031663 (print) | LCCN 2022031664 (ebook) | ISBN 9781032396521 (paperback) | ISBN 9781003350743 (ebook)
Subjects: LCSH: Autistic children--Care | Parents of autistic children--Handbooks, manuals, etc.
Classification: LCC RJ506.A9 D84 2023 (print) | LCC RJ506.A9 (ebook) |
DDC 618.92/85882--dc23/eng/20220928
LC record available at https://lccn.loc.gov/2022031663
LC ebook record available at https://lccn.loc.gov/2022031664

ISBN: 978-1-032-39652-1 (pbk)
ISBN: 978-1-003-35074-3 (ebk)

DOI: 10.4324/9781003350743

Typeset in Verdana
by Deanta Global Publishing Services, Chennai, India

Access the companion website: https://resourcecentre.routledge.com/speechmark

Printed in Great Britain by Bell and Bain Ltd, Glasgow

For Leroy Duffus, Karen Shaw, Gunny Lenz-Mulligan and Janet Wilson: you would have loved this. Your legacies live on.

CONTENTS

"Autism is a tool that can be used to open almost anything – you've just got to know how to use it. Sometimes an autistic person needs somebody to discover who they really are as sometimes they can't find it for themselves. Autism needs watering – it's like a seed that's had no water, but once it's been watered, all of a sudden, the flower that comes out has never been seen before – it's the most beautiful flower ever seen on the planet."

Willard Wigan MBE

ACKNOWLEDGEMENTS

This book wouldn't have been possible without the input from so many amazing autistic young people. Special thanks go to Pavan and Talhah for contributing and advising on content, and to James, Ali, Lucas, Nabeel, Thérèse, Holly, Daniel, Fatima, Grace, Daisy, Jada and Dylan for providing such a range of ideas that shaped these books. Thanks also go to Roberta Heys and Moyna Talcer for providing content and advice.

Likewise, I have been so grateful for input from amazing individuals such as Carly Jones MBE, Willard Wigan MBE, Emily Katy, Holly Smale, Dan Jones, Chris Baker, Lynn McCann, Claire Prosser and Andrew Whitehouse. Your emails, calls and twitter DMs have made this process even more enjoyable. A special mention should go to Luke Beardon, my Masters supervisor from back in 2017, who put an extra fire in my belly to make a difference in this PNT-focused world.

I have been very lucky to be offered so many opportunities by both Sutton Council and Cognus Limited, and to have worked with some amazing colleagues. Working with so many young people, families and schools has been a gift and has taught me so much. This has been particularly enhanced by my time working with Melanie Vijayaratnam and Tracy Matthews (now running Adapt to Learn), Fernando Teixido-Infante (Intensive Interaction extraordinaire) and Isabell Fisher (now running Little Hands Learning).

There is an amazing school that I regularly work with, and it has a very special place in my heart. Duvessa and Asma, thank you for all your enthusiasm and encouragement: my cheerleaders! Apologies: this is starting to feel like an Oscar acceptance speech…!

To my illustrator, Beth, from Winters Bee Studios. So many emails – I'm sorry! Your contribution to the books has been invaluable.

To the team at Routledge Education for all your help; in particular, my editor Clare Ashworth, and assistant editor, Molly Kavanagh, for seeing the potential for this book and supporting me along the way.

To Pam and Tony: the original proof-readers. It's a real act of love when you are prepared to spend your retirement discussing your daughter's use of commas.

You gave me the most wonderful childhood (still ongoing if we're honest!) and my love of books began with you.

To Brian. I owe you a lot of domestic chores! I know how lucky I am to have found my soulmate. Thank you for always being there for me through the ups and downs of life and helping me to believe in myself.

I hope these books help others to recognise and believe in their own value and what they bring to the world.

Chapter 1

INTRODUCTION

As a specialist advisory teacher for autism, I have worked with hundreds of young people, supporting them to better understand their autistic identity. Over the years, I have developed different techniques to enhance these conversations, and people often ask me about them. My motivation for creating these books was to ensure that more young people have access to positive conversations around their autistic identity, and they are empowered to make life choices that ensure they build on their strengths. To facilitate that, I realised I needed to create both a workbook for the young person to personalise, and a guidance book for the adult involved. This became about empowering the family around the young person, and by that, I mean the whole unit of parents/carers, wider family members and school staff.

The creation of these resources has been shaped and polished by autistic individuals, from young people who have shared their own experiences through quotes embedded in the book, to the focus groups of students who offered feedback and suggestions, to adult autistic reviewers. I hope that as a young person works through this resource, they feel a sense of their voice adding to their autistic 'tribe'.

This book is designed to be worked through as an activity for the young person, (with some help from an adult) to understand and explore the different ideas. You, as the adult, may be the parent or carer of the young person, or perhaps a member of staff from the young person's school. Throughout the book I will refer to 'guiding' the young person through the workbook. Your role here is to escort or accompany them through this initial part of the process of understanding their identity. This process will be theirs through their life – their own journey of understanding – and you are helping them on the path.

DOI: 10.4324/9781003350743-1

"The understanding diagnosis sessions with Rebecca were absolutely key to our family and to my son. They were the first time in the whole process of assessment and diagnosis that anyone had really spoken directly to the child and in words and language tailored to them, in a way that they might understand and could ask questions and explore. It's the first step in what can be a very long journey of self-acceptance. It was the first time there had been a discussion that autism might be a positive thing, or at least not an entirely negative thing. Up until that point it was always couched in 'something being wrong or different' and the conversations the child is involved in are never directed to the child, they are directed to the parents, carers, the teachers around them… and of course, they are going to be worried, thinking 'well what's wrong with me?' So, this book is the first step in the child-centred approach to explaining that diagnosis, explaining how their brain works to them and how they fit in with the rest of their peers, in society, and the benefits they can bring to their friends and their environment." – **Roberta (Parent)**

Purpose

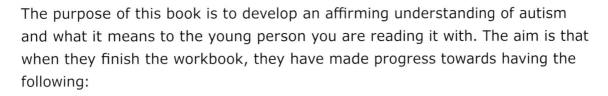

"This is excellent as it's hard to always put into words and explain yourself to someone. It's yours, it's personalised to you, and it really gets over that barrier where people fall on that one stereotype of autism. People don't realise it's not just one thing."
– **Talhah**

The purpose of this book is to develop an affirming understanding of autism and what it means to the young person you are reading it with. The aim is that when they finish the workbook, they have made progress towards having the following:

- An understanding of what autism is.

- An understanding of what autism means to them (their autistic identity).

- A positive sense of self.

- An acknowledgement of things that may be trickier.

- A pride in being autistic.

A sense of self, or an understanding of who you are and how you best operate, is something that many people strive for throughout their lives. It often changes over time, based on what is happening to you, and around you at each stage in your life. Therefore, we would be naive to think that one workbook would achieve a positive self-identity… tick, job done! If only it were that simple… However, this is the starting point. This is the start of many more conversations throughout the individual's life. The foundations. The building blocks. Whatever imagery works for you, keep that in your head. After the final page is finished, the job isn't done. Unfortunately, I can't give you a resource list for the future, but I can tell you that resources are multiplying as we speak. If you head to Twitter and search for the hashtags #actuallyautistic and #askautistics, you will find many insightful threads from autistic individuals sharing their points of view and accounts of their experiences. These are great both for the young person to read as they get older, and for those around them to gain insights and use as discussion points.

A few recommendations I can make are:

- Continue the conversation, and not always verbally: use links, articles, and videos.

- Follow their lead – you want to develop autistic pride, but it is very important to respect their communication preferences. Do they want to share their workbook with other family members and friends, or perhaps just their 'autism identity statement'? Is this something they want to talk about all the time or just with specific people in school and at home?

- Visual information is often easier to process, so encourage them to watch/follow autistic YouTubers such as 'The Aspie World', 'Purple Ella' and 'Charl Davies'.

- Use the workbook in the way that works for them. They may want to keep coming back to it or develop their own ongoing workbooks. Consider buying personalised notebooks or encourage them to set up their own system to help process information on an ongoing basis. This could be recording voice notes, videos or typing into a document.

A parent's perspective

Thoughts and feelings through the identification process

"It was a relief to receive the diagnosis – a sense of feeling finally being listened to, of validation of concerns and a sense that finally some help for my son, and for us, was coming. It wasn't a surprise for us as it had been a long journey to get to this stage, with my son expressing suicidal intent at age 6, before we were able to access help. It felt like we had to fight to overcome huge hurdles at each stage just to get someone to help and to listen. It's a very, very scary place, as parents we put our faith and trust in professionals, but that faith and trust is so often challenged and broken, so by the time of diagnosis, it felt like the cavalry was coming to help! Of course, this was tinged with regret at not being able to have understood or helped my son earlier, and sadness at knowing that his life was going to be different to how we might have imagined. But given how bad things had got before diagnosis, we had already hit rock bottom and felt hopeless. So, a diagnosis gave us hope.

It's important to say that in cases such as these, parents miss out the step of being supported to understand, accept and come to terms with the fact their child is autistic – all those feelings are largely pushed away or not dealt with as the main focus is on getting help and getting someone to listen to concerns that you are not a bad parent or that the child isn't simply 'naughty'."
– Roberta

Talking to my child about their autistic identity

"My son was included and involved at every stage of diagnosis and assessment and at age 6 was old enough to follow conversations, however, there were no direct communications with him as a child by professionals, so until Rebecca's programme, this was left to us as parents to manage directly with our son. On the day of diagnosis, we talked to our son about what was happening and what the doctors had said, and we knew enough about autism ourselves to start to have the conversation from very early on.

We had done our own research using resources from the National Autistic Society and reading recommended books and literature. When we had help from Rebecca, we followed her advice, and tried to move with our son at his own pace, mindful of not overwhelming him and mindful of his mental health state, which was fragile at the time. It wasn't a one-off process – he's 15 now, and we are – and he is – still on the journey of understanding and processing." – **Roberta**

Things you should and shouldn't say

"It's very hard I think to put a really positive upbeat spin on autism for a child who has had to go through years of exclusion and pain, becoming suicidal, with parents going from pillar to post to find out not what is wrong, but how to help their child, only to have to fight at every turn before finally getting a diagnosis – I think it's going to be very difficult psychologically for some in that situation to then accept autism as a positive, rather as a thing that is 'wrong'. It very much depends on the journey and the personality of the child on how to approach the framing. For some, it might work really well to accentuate autistic pride right from the start, but for others, a recognition of the trauma they have been through already might dictate an approach which acknowledges the trauma and builds slowly. As with everything where humans are concerned, there is no one size that fits all." – **Roberta**

Chapter 2

BACKGROUND INFORMATION

Social and medical models of disability

Historically, the process of getting an autism diagnosis is a very 'medicalised' process. You generally have to go to a medical institution, such as a hospital or clinic, and you are seen by a medical professional. A medical diagnostic manual is used, full of medicalised language, talking about 'disorders' and 'deficits'.

Over time, mainly fuelled by autistic adults, this process has been challenged. Many diagnostic waiting lists are extremely long (as I'm sure you are well aware!) and some autistic adults are self-identifying rather than bearing the agonising wait to be assessed. As there is no singular 'test' for autism, this poses the questions: should we be talking about autism being identified rather than diagnosed and would some autistic 'deficits' really be deficits if it weren't for the challenges society poses?

Let me elaborate... Imagine a wheelchair user who is unable to access the platform at a train station. Are they being excluded from this situation because of their disability, or because the station does not have step-free access? Consider an autistic young person at school who doesn't have any friends and lacks social connections. Have they been excluded because of their disability or because of lack of support in the setting and from their peer group? Is it their differences in social communication that are the barrier, or the lack of education and understanding from the group around them?

The social model of disability suggests that we should understand disability from the wider perspective of society as a whole, rather than focusing on the differences within that individual. Many of these so-called 'deficits' are in fact

DOI: 10.4324/9781003350743-2

opportunities for support and adaptations to be made by the immediate network (e.g., family, friends, school, work etc.) and the wider network (government policies etc.). For example, the wheelchair user is no longer excluded from the setting when there is step-free access. Likewise, the autistic student is able to develop social connections when provided with a supportive peer group and opportunities suited to their interests.

Why am I telling you all this? It is important to be abreast of developments in the understanding of disability, and these principles underpin the whole of this book. Your child/young person is likely to develop a more positive self-identity if they understand their place in wider society. If they understand these barriers, they may be able to advocate for themselves and ask for adjustments, and 'call out' those barriers when adjustments are not in place, without feeling guilty for doing so.

This is not to dismiss the difficulties that autistic individuals often face on a daily basis, but it does try to focus on where many of these barriers come from, shifting the 'blame' away from the individual and onto the structural hurdles in society as a whole.

Neurodiversity

We would not be where we are as a society if we didn't have lots of different ways of processing and perceiving the world. Diversity in thinking is an asset and this school of thought is known as neurodiversity.

Neurodiversity is the term used to describe the many ways that our brains learn and process information about the world. The main premise of this movement is that this is a natural part of human diversity. In the same way that we celebrate ethnic diversity, neurological diversity should also be understood and celebrated as part of human variation.

Individuals who take the pathway of neurological development that is seen as 'typical', or that most people are understood to follow, are known as **'neurotypical'**, or to be the 'predominant neurotype'.

Individuals whose brains process in different, equally good ways, are known as **'neurodivergent'** e.g., those who are autistic, ADHD or dyslexic, for example.

Terminology

Throughout this book, I aim to use terminology that is seen by the wider autistic community as autism-affirming. The list below is by no means exhaustive, but gives a good starting point for some terms to be wary of, and possible suitable alternatives.

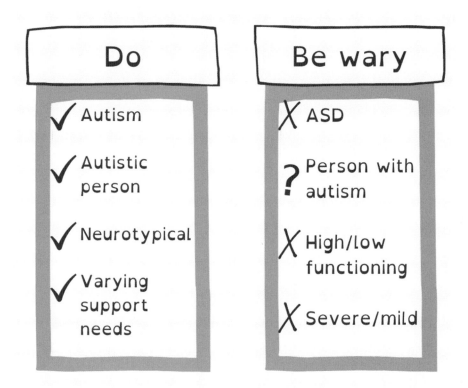

Do	Be wary
✓ Autism	✗ ASD
✓ Autistic person	? Person with autism
✓ Neurotypical	✗ High/low functioning
✓ Varying support needs	✗ Severe/mild

Autism/ASD

- The acronym ASD stands for autism spectrum disorder, which comes from the medical diagnostic manual (therefore following the medical model). The word 'disorder' focuses on deficits. Many young people will have an official diagnosis of ASD, however this does not mean we need to continue to use this language (therefore reinforcing negative stereotypes) when we talk about this aspect of their identity. For some reason, we seem to love an acronym, and so people have tried to re-define the letters or introduce alternative acronyms to represent autism. My belief is that the word autism does the job very well. Yes, it's three syllables, but it's a short enough word and does not contain negative bias.

Autistic person/person with autism

- Research into terms used to describe autism (Kenny et al., 2016), found that identity-first language (autistic person) was preferable to person-first (person with autism), however it should be noted that this is an individual preference, and so the most important thing to remember is to always ask the individual.

High/low functioning and severe/mild

- Functioning labels tend to result in those labelled as 'high functioning' not getting the support they need, and those labelled as 'low functioning' not being given access to opportunities.

- In addition, the labels themselves are inaccurate – what are they measuring? How able you are to function in different situations? Well surely that depends on the situation, the people involved, what support is on offer, how you are feeling, if you've had a good lunch beforehand etc. etc.? In reality, this often ends up referring to someone's intellectual ability, which is unrelated to their autistic identity.

- These labels are effectively ways of neurotypicals making sense of autism and trying to measure it against non-autistic ways of functioning. As Yenn Purkis explains, "they essentially say, 'how normal are you?'" (Purkis, 2017).

- Instead, a suitable alternative would be to refer to someone's strengths and support needs, which would vary depending on the circumstances.

Chapter 3

WHAT IS AUTISM?

Definitions of autism are regularly changing, and that's a good thing! Our understanding of autism is growing because autistic individuals are sharing their own experiences and stories. Research into different aspects of autism is also increasing, for example, exploring why someone's gender, ethnicity or where they live may impact access to an autism diagnosis.

This reiterates the importance of encouraging a positive sense of self, as these positive foundations remain constant as the definitions change.

Monotropism

Over the years, there have been many theories that attempt to 'explain' autism. Many have been challenged or only serve to explain certain elements of an autistic person's identity.

However, one theory, the theory of monotropism, introduced by Dinah Murray (1992), is widely seen as being one of the best explanations for the autistic way of being.

This theory suggests that there are two different ways of processing information and approaching the world:

- Monotropic.
- Polytropic.

DOI: 10.4324/9781003350743-3

Individuals who have monotropic minds will often be focused on single channels of attention (or attention tunnels), to a deeper level. Those who are polytropic tend to have multiple channels of attention, but these are shallower. This theory is thought of as one of the most successful for explaining autistic ways of thinking and processing, because it explains the differences in social interaction, focus on interests and sensory processing.

Let's go into each of these in more detail...

An autism assessment

When a young person is diagnosed as autistic, this is done by a medical professional, following what is known as the 'medical(ised) model' of disability. This means the process is quite highly focused on 'deficits' and often uses language that portrays autism in a negative light.

A diagnosis is generally given of ASD, which stands for 'autism spectrum disorder'. For the individual or parents, this is immediately damaging towards their understanding of their identity. To be told you have a 'disorder' chips away at your self-esteem and often reinforces any negative thoughts you already had. (You'll find this high up in the 'things not to say' section!)

Diagnostic processes are changing and in some settings there is a move towards a more social model of disability (see previous section) – seeing difference as something to be celebrated.

If you are interested in the exact wording of the medicalised diagnostic criteria, a simple online search will take you there.

Here I will focus on a 'social model' interpretation of autism.

Social differences

Examples include:

- May prefer alternative forms of communication to verbal. May find talking to people trickier, generally with those that they do not know well.

"Talking to other people makes me anxious sometimes but if I'm used to them, I will let out all my feelings. If it's a new person I'm like 'where do I start'?" – **Grace**

- May prefer to work alone rather than in a group.

- Playing games that do not have clear rules may be difficult. For example, with informal football where the teams adjust the rules based on the situation, it may be difficult to adapt to these unpredictable changes.

- May prefer somewhere quieter over busy places, e.g., may choose the school library over the busy playground at break times.

- Conversations may be a source of anxiety: it may be difficult to know when to speak, when to stop, whether someone else is interested etc.

- Different communication styles: may be very skilled when presenting or speaking about interests but find it more difficult when there's a two-way interaction or lack of visual support.

- May find it difficult to read body language and facial expressions or may not make the body language or facial expressions other people 'expect'.

- Loyalty and vulnerability: may be very honest and expect the same from others which can lead to others taking advantage.

- Listening to lots of verbal input: may find it tricky to process communication that is solely verbal, e.g., the teacher talking for long periods without the support of any visual stimuli to back up what they are saying.

> *"I find it hard to listen to lots of talking. In class I would be thinking about when I would be going outside or when I would be going home so then I would zone out with all the questions in my head or daydream."* – **Fatima**

- Not modifying behaviour depending on the person they are interacting with, e.g., may behave in the same way with the headteacher as with their mates in the playground, rather than adapting to the situation/context.

Interests and focus

- May have interests that are different from peers.

- Can be fully immersed in interests and block out everything else going on around.

- May spend longer than average absorbed in interests and therefore may become experts in the topic.

- Interests are not 'stuck' and will change over time, but the intensity is greater than neurotypical peers.

- May have an amazing memory for certain things, usually something that has engaged their interests.

"I've got a good attention for some things – I will remember details and specific memories. I'll feel like I was there in the moment again. They don't seem to fade over time – I just collect more."
– Jada

- May be able to imagine things in pictures in the mind, e.g., in a maths lesson they may be able to work out the answer in their mind and then not bother with any workings out (which seem pointless if you can do it in your head!)

- May be able to immerse themselves in their own imagination and use this as a source of amusement or as a calming strategy.

- May find it difficult to shift attention from one thing to another (whether a topic, part of the lesson or activity, e.g., shifting from homework to dinner time). This may be because they are engrossed in the initial task and are not ready to move on or have not had prior warning and find the transition unexpected.

- May have difficulties with organisation such as sequencing the steps required within a task, e.g., completing a homework project. May also find personal organisation tricky, e.g., remembering what resources are needed for each lesson across the school week.

- May be able to focus on small details that others miss.

"In movies, I focus on an object that is in the background. I wonder what will happen to it when the movie moves on. Sometimes I focus on the object too much and then miss an important scene." **– Nabeel**

Routine and structure

- Liking having a predictable structure and wanting to know the plan in advance.

- Finding it difficult if things change, e.g., a different teacher or something is cancelled.

- Needing time to recharge or recover after lots of social or sensory input.

Chapter 4

SENSORY DIFFERENCES

This chapter has been written in consultation with Moyna Talcer, neurodivergent Consultant Occupational Therapist.

We all process the world through our senses. There are five basic senses that we are often aware of. But did you know there are many different senses that work together to shape the information that our brain processes about the world?

We are going to focus on eight key senses which are relevant to our young people:

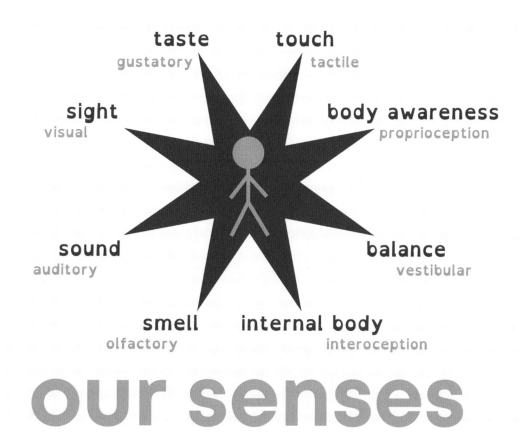

DOI: 10.4324/9781003350743-4

Sensory processing

Information from our senses travels to our brain, where it is processed for meaning. In a very basic form, it works like this:

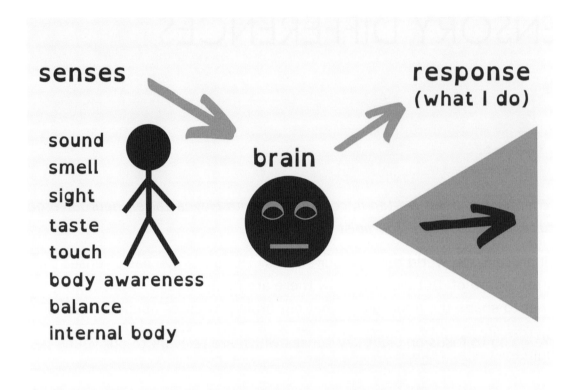

For everyone interpreting sensory information, there will be individual differences. Think about a time you have shared a space with other people, perhaps an office, classroom or living room. It is very rare for your temperature requirements to all be completely in sync. Usually someone is flinging all the windows open, while others are reaching to turn the thermostat up! Other examples include different preferences for spice levels, clothing fabrics, lighting levels and bedding types (some people like heavy bedding all year round, others can sleep without anything covering them).

With autistic individuals, or those with sensory processing differences, these differences are often more extreme and can have an impact on your day-to-day functioning.

If the smell of food wafting from the canteen is too overwhelming, you will find it difficult to focus in class, or if the overhead lights are flickering, it can make your eyes hurt and cause difficulty focusing on the task at hand. If you're in a busy shopping mall with lots of competing different noises like people talking, the sounds of music playing from different stores and constant overhead announcements being made to shoppers, it can leave you feeling utterly drained and overwhelmed.

These examples are of potentially negative points, but for others, some responses can be a source of real joy.

Listening to your favourite music track on repeat, lighting your favourite scented candle or incense, or wearing your favourite fabrics can bring about a sense of relaxation and peace. For others, experiencing certain types of repetitive movement such as rocking, swinging or jumping can bring a sense of balance and calm and even joy. These experiences are often referred to as stimming, which are important for self-regulation and releasing stress and anxiety.

Tapping into the joy of movement can help an individual to feel grounded.

Sensory sensitivity

Research has found that for each of the eight senses mentioned above, 96% of autistic individuals will experience sensory processing differences (Marco et al., 2011). This may be over-reactivity, under-reactivity or fluctuating-reactivity (changing between the two).

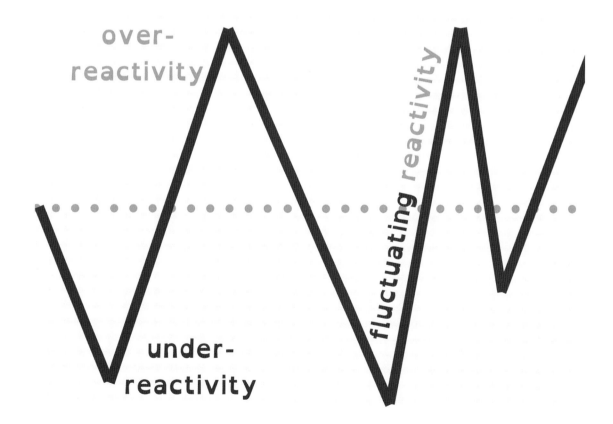

Now just to keep you on your toes, the extra tricky bit is that reactions to sensory stimuli are not always predictable, and they can change! Think of a time when you were especially tired and just wanted to have a rest, but someone wanted to talk to you, or a time when you felt unwell and were having to focus on a difficult topic. I'm sure in those moments, your ability to engage would have been less than optimal. It's the same for autistic people. If you are tired, ill, anxious or things in your environment are changing, this can all affect your thresholds for tolerance.

> *"I find spicy food unbearable. But I really like a certain brand of extra hot crisps. There's something about the taste being predictable and me knowing what I'm going to get."* – **Talhal**

I remember working with a young person who found it really difficult to cope with certain sounds. An African Drumming workshop was coming to the school the next day and the staff were quite concerned about how this learner would react. Well… he loved it!

The thing for him was that he couldn't stand unexpected sounds, like those from the computer when there is a quiz, and someone gets an answer right or wrong. But when the sounds were in his control (he was hitting the drum), and were of a lower pitch and frequency, he quite enjoyed them. Control and predictability play a big part here, as they do with most areas related to autism.

The eight senses in detail

Sight (visual)

Many autistic individuals are visual learners and can process visual information more quickly than, for example, verbal information.

It is important to refer to eye contact here. This is something that neurotypical individuals can get a bit obsessed with… When I go into schools I often see 'good looking' signs dotted around the place, but who defines whether that is necessary (and what it even means?!)? For some autistic people, they explain that giving eye contact can at worst be painful, and at best detract from their understanding of what the other person is saying. If we think back to the monotropism theory (or single attention tunnel), it can be very difficult to process both someone's face/body language, AND what they are saying.

> *"I find it easier to look at the whiteboard or thing the teacher is reading from rather than looking at the teacher. I don't really like giving eye contact. When I'm asked to track the speaker, I look for a few seconds and then look away as I feel uncomfortable."*
> — **Nabeel**

The message here is simple, don't insist on eye contact and don't equate eye contact with listening. Be aware that when the individual feels that this is expected of them, it may impact on their processing of information. The best approach is to empower the individual to be able to advocate for themselves.

> *"When I have a new teacher, I will try to tell them that I listen in a different way and I'm not being rude. It's written on my IEP (Individual Education Plan), but I feel better if I tell them myself as then I know that they know."* — **Pavan**

Differences with processing in this area may mean:

- Ability to focus on small details.
- Flicking fingers in front of eyes for visual stimulation or to block out other visual input.
- Difficulty concentrating in visually 'busy' environments, e.g., classroom with things stuck on every inch of the walls and with things dangling from the ceiling.

- Preferring low lighting or bright lighting.

- Liking to turn lights on and off.

- Enjoying the visual movement of sprinkling, decanting, throwing, lining up or dropping objects.

- Looking out of the corner of the eyes (peripheral) – this sometimes leads to people thinking the individual hasn't looked at something, e.g., the visual timetable, when in fact they have glanced out of their peripheral vision and quickly processed all the information required.

- Liking the environment to look a certain way, e.g., drawers all closed, doors closed, curtains just so and objects lined up or placed exactly in the correct position.

> *"For me, as an adult, I need my visual environment to be predictable, tidy, and neat. This is very hard to achieve with a 'fizzy' 7-year-old, and two rescue dogs who like to scatter their belongings all over the place. I set up rituals and routines relating to my environment, and these help me feel calm."* – **Moyna**

Sound (auditory)

This follows on nicely from the visual sense. Remember, if auditory processing is the aim (such as understanding verbal information), don't insist on looking as well as listening – decide what the key sensory focus needs to be.

Differences with processing in this area may mean:

- Can be sensitive to certain sounds – covers ears to try and block them out or prefers to wear ear defenders/ear plugs.

- Hums or sings to screen out noises.

- Puts ear close to noises to listen.

- Enjoys the same sounds on repeat.

- Difficulties locating sounds.

"I used to love the sound of a puzzle piece going into the wooden hole. I would hold it up to my ear and put it in over and over again." – **Fatima**

"I find it extremely difficult to focus when there are any background noises. When I was studying for my degree, I had to close my study door, turn my mobile off, and ask the other house members to go out for the day. If they didn't, I was unable to focus and if I was reading a research article and they made a sound, I would immediately be distracted, then forget what I had read and have to start again. It was extremely effortful and stressful. I have learnt to use ear plugs to silence the outside world and also use my overhead headphones for added sound buffering." – **Moyna**

Pavan explains:

Autistic person: "It's too loud!"

Neurotypical: "Other people are able to cope so you can cope too."

Everyone copes differently. Neurotypicals have got to understand that the way they cope with sensory aspects isn't the same as the way autistic people cope with them.

Smell (olfactory)

The sense of smell is closely linked with the sense of taste. This is a powerful sense as its neurological connections go straight to the brain and have a strong link to our emotions and memories.

"*Think of a positive time from your past, for me it was always the sweet spicy smell of those delicious chocolate glazed Lebkuchen biscuits that my Irish grandmother used to give to my sister and I at Easter. Every time I smell them, my mind goes back to those special moments, and it instantly makes me feel safe, warm, and content. Conversely, I also recall a negative association with smells when my father used to grill mackerel every single Sunday morning for his breakfast, I found the smell utterly overpowering and could smell it on my hair, clothing, and skin for the entire day. I now can't eat fish as I have this strong negative association with this smell. Smells can help us feel instantly calm, safe, and relaxed, but they can also trigger us, so it's important that we know what smells we like and what smells we dislike so we can be better aware.*" – **Moyna**

Differences with processing in this area may mean:

- Can have strong preferences or dislike particular smells.
- May sniff people, objects or food to assess the situation or gain pleasure (e.g., may be able to identify who the lost jumper belongs to by smelling it).
- Holds nose to avoid certain smells.

"*I love strong smells especially perfume but sometimes it can be a bit too much. Hand sanitiser is way too strong and makes my nose tingle when I smell it. It smells plain but strong. Why can't it smell like roses?*" – **Grace**

Taste (gustatory)

As mentioned previously, sense of taste is closely linked with the sense of smell. It also links with visual processing as some individuals may find it difficult if food is presented in a different way, or if food is touching on a plate.

Differences with processing in this area may mean:

- Might be described as a 'fussy eater' or have a limited diet.

- Will only eat certain flavours, colours or textures such as 'beige foods/carbs'.

- Finds it challenging to try new foods.

- Spots small changes in recipes or when a secret vegetable has been slipped in!

- May notice the change in taste if items are stored in plastic containers.

- May be able to detect that the food item was purchased from a different shop or made by a different brand.

"I don't like how kids' plastic cups feel on my tongue – it spoils the taste." – **Fatima**

"I am particularly fussy about the taste of my coffee. I cannot stand the flavour of Starbucks coffee, but like the bitterness of Nero and Costa. I also hate the taste of full-fat milk in my coffee and can taste if the barista has forgotten my order." – **Moyna**

Pavan explains:

Autistic people aren't 'selective eaters', 'picky eaters' or 'fussy eaters'. It's sensory hell that stops autistic people from wanting to eat certain foods and that's not their fault.

Them: "You ate this fruit last week so why can't you eat it today, it's the same thing!"

It's not. For example, there are two strawberries. One strawberry is sour, and one is sweet. Yes, they're both strawberries but why don't I want to eat one of them? Because it's sour!

Touch (tactile)

Unexpected touch or certain tactile sensations can lead to distress or cause upset. In contrast, under-reaction to touch may make the individual seem unresponsive.

I remember working with a young person who would often say that people had hit her. Adults around her couldn't understand what was going on, as they would witness situations and see with their 'own eyes' (and own perception!) that she hadn't been hit. However, for this girl, the tickles, or gentle touches she was receiving were being experienced as painful sensations, due to the way her brain processed the information. For her, a firm touch felt much more comfortable than a light 'tickly' sensation.

Differences with processing in this area may mean:

- Likes firm massage/squeezing/hugs (links with body awareness sense).
- Can be very sensitive to touch – this can impact other people's expectations of social interaction as they may avoid hugs and close contact.
- Finds dressing very stressful.
- Avoids bare feet.
- Doesn't like sensation of wearing shoes and socks.
- Cuts out labels and tags.
- May put objects in the mouth.
- Chews on sleeves or collars.
- Prefers old clothing or comfier garments.
- Avoids gluing, painting, and sand play.
- Is always seeking to touch things.
- Loves messy activities.
- Does not notice if there's food still in the mouth after eating.

> *"I don't like fancy dress. It feels like it bites you."* – **Fatima**
>
> *"I like to have something to fiddle with – I might use a pen or my hands if I have no fidget tool."* – **Ali**
>
> *"It was really annoying that my most treasured possession, my Wimbledon shirt, had a really big itchy label on it."* – **James**
>
> *"I cannot wear jeans; the material is too harsh and stiff, and I feel like I'm in a strait jacket. I hated wearing tights for my entire childhood, as an adult I have learnt to choose tights with a soft silky feel with a thick and soft waistband."* – **Moyna**

Body awareness (proprioception)

Proprioception is the hidden sense that tells us where our body parts are, without the use of vision.

There are receptors in our muscles and joints, and they respond to movement, telling us where our body parts are in relation to each other and things around us. For example, if you asked me to close my eyes and describe where my body parts were, I could tell you that I have my legs crossed at the ankles, my wrists resting on the desk and my fingers touching the keyboard. I wouldn't need to look to gain that information, as my proprioceptive sense is sending those messages to my brain. However, with another example, I might have a sip from a glass of water and as I go to put it back on the desk, I knock over other things on my desk, and put the glass down with slightly too much force, causing it to spill. If you have difficulties with proprioception, understanding your physical place in the world, as well as in relation to other objects, can be tricky. Together with tactile discrimination, the proprioceptive sense helps us do things such as do up our top buttons, tie an apron behind our back, brush the hair at the back of our head, do up a clasp on our necklace or put in earrings without looking in a mirror.

Differences with processing in this area may mean:

- Has difficulty using the correct force for tasks such as pouring a glass of water without spilling, or writing without your marks going through to the other side.

- Seems clumsy.

- Heavy footed.

- Heavy handed.

- Difficulties with fine and gross motor skills.

- Bumps into things.

> *"When I pour myself a drink, I always seem to spill it!"* – **Fatima**
>
> *"I am covered in bruises and can never recall where they came from. I seem to walk into door frames and furniture all the time."*
> – **Moyna**

Balance (vestibular)

The vestibular sense is your sense of balance and is closely linked to the ears and the eyes (if you've ever tried to stand on one leg with your eyes closed, you will know this! And if you haven't, I don't know why not, but go on… try it now!)

The vestibular sense is what helps keep you upright when standing on a train, or after bending down to pick up a pen off the floor. It also helps you orientate to which way is up if you dive into a pool.

Differences with processing in this area may mean:

- Enjoys the sensation of rocking back and forth.

- Enjoys spinning – can be indulged in without getting dizzy.

- Seeks out experiences that challenge feelings of stability and balance, e.g., roller coasters.

- Craves 'risky' sensations – balancing on thin supports or climbing to the top of precarious heights.

- Can be slower at changing direction of movement when running.

- Finds it difficult to maintain speed.

- Finds it trickier walking and balancing.

- Avoids experiences that accentuate feelings of dizziness, e.g., balancing or roller coasters.

- Finds it difficult to sit up straight at a desk.

- Sits in a 'W' shape (knees in front, ankles and feet to the side).

- Can avoid moving the head when bending over.

- May get motion sick in the car.

- Avoids movement-based activities such as PE, sports or other such tasks and prefers sedentary activities.

- Gets dizzy easily.

Internal body (interoception)

The interoceptive sense is your internal body sense, which helps you understand what's going on inside you. It includes physical sensations related to bodily functions as well as how you are feeling emotionally. Interoception is essentially the internal version of proprioception.

Differences with processing in this area may mean you struggle to recognise the physical sensations of emotions or to know whether:

- You need the toilet.

- You are hungry or are full up.

- You are hot or cold.

- You are thirsty.

- You are unwell.

- You are itchy.

> *"I didn't know I needed to go to the toilet every day – my mum had to tell me."* – **Daisy**
>
> *"I have no idea if I am sick, tired, hungry or frightened, the sensation feels the same and it makes me really anxious."* – **Jada**
>
> *"I never feel hungry, and often forget to eat."* – **Pavan**
>
> *"I never feel the need to drink. I need to be reminded all the time or I will go days without drinking any fluids."* – **Grace**

Processing differences may mean emotions are interpreted (or not interpreted) in different ways from the majority. Some individuals may not realise they are feeling scared/fear because they don't identify the physical cues in their body (sweating, heart beating faster, breathing becomes shallow etc.). Likewise, other individuals may find it difficult to distinguish between feeling anxious, feeling sick, needing the toilet or feeling hungry. All involve sensations in the stomach region, but our interpretation of these senses is often highly context driven.

> *"I didn't realise other people feel the same way I do. I thought my tummy ache meant I was really ill but then I ate something, and it went away. I realised I was just hungry."* – **Jada**

Sensory overload

Sometimes, the amount of sensory information a person experiences can just be too much. It can feel overwhelming to experience so much detail at once, and they may experience physical sensations such as a headache, feeling sick, feeling dizzy or sweating.

Often it can help to take some time out, in a lower arousal setting. This may be outside where there is more space and things are usually further away, or it may be in a darker area where there is less visual input.

Meltdown

> *"Autistic meltdowns aren't 'attention seeking'. It may look like they're 'screaming for attention' but they aren't screaming for attention, they're screaming because they want all the sensory hell or the emotional hell to stop altogether."* – **Pavan**

Meltdowns are not solely caused by sensory overwhelm, but this can often be a contributing factor. Alongside emotional distress, or anxiety, everything can feel like 'too much'.

Think of a time when your senses were heightened – perhaps when you were unwell, or feeling particularly tired. Then, imagine that you had to go to a busy exhibition centre, full of people, blaring music and a cocktail of smells. You're wearing something particularly uncomfortable and are starving hungry. People are trying to grab your attention and get you to buy something from their brightly coloured stalls. Oh, and you're bursting for the toilet! This is an extreme example, but it is hopefully easy to imagine why you might need to just get out of there (via the WC!) and recover. This is what a sensory meltdown can be like for autistic individuals. In situations of extreme stress, our body goes into fight or flight stress responses. 'Flight' translates to, 'get out of there', but this isn't always possible, and so we are left with 'fight'. Outbursts of extreme stress are known as autistic meltdowns. The individual has usually lost control of rational thought and an understanding of the consequences of their actions. The actions are not deliberate, and this should not be confused with a 'tantrum'. As the adult with the young person at this time, this is important to remember, as we can have a tendency to make it about ourselves. I'm afraid to tell you, on this occasion, it isn't all about you!

Responses to meltdowns should focus on keeping the individual safe, with as little input as possible. Now is not the time to be reasoning with the young person or trying to give additional sensory input. You will know your child, or the young person you are working with, far better than I do, so tap into what you know about them – what do they find calming and what has helped in the past?

It is usually best to say less, and do less, but some individuals may find deep pressure or firm touch very calming – know your young person.

Shutdown

Following on from the fight or flight response, the third option is 'freeze'. This is also known as an autistic shutdown. Like the meltdown, it can be caused by overwhelming sensory information or situations that are demanding socially, emotionally, cognitively or physically.

Think of a computer shutting down – if you're anything like me, you don't turn off your computer anywhere near as much as you should. However, when left for long periods in 'sleep' mode, without the opportunity to recharge, and with more and more demands placed on the device, eventually it will stop being able to perform all the required commands and just focus on basic functions. This is similar to an autistic shutdown. The individual is at a reduced capacity to process and interact with the world around them, and so they may retreat, having minimal communication. As with meltdowns, the reaction to a shutdown should be to give the individual space to 'reboot', without putting additional demands on them.

With shutdowns, it is particularly important to be aware of those young people who are seen as 'shy' or 'quiet'. Information gathering is key here – are they 'shy' and 'quiet' in other situations, or are they actually just struggling to get through the day with the demands being placed on them?

> *"The autistic person can be suffering and struggling so much in the sensory environment but be masking and suffering in silence."*
> **– Pavan**

Throughout the book, we will look at strategies that can be personalised to the young person you are working with, but here are a few general ideas that can help with meltdowns and shutdowns:

• Keep a log of triggers.

• Be proactive rather than reactive – try to plan ahead to avoid triggers.

• Add predictability – provide information in advance about what to expect, e.g., a visual timetable or schedule.

• Provide sensory regulation tools, e.g., ear defenders.

• Adapt the sensory environment, e.g., dim the lights.

• Speak to the individual – find out what they feel the causes are and what would help them.

Chapter 5

EMOTIONS, ANXIETY AND MASKING

Emotions

Understanding emotions is a difficult concept for everyone – how many adults do you know who have all their emotions 'sorted'?! In fact, the very aim to have them 'sorted', can be part of the problem.

We all experience a range of emotions in our lifetime (or even day) and this is normal. No one is happy all of the time. Seeing some emotions as 'good' and others as 'bad', doesn't help here. Sometimes the aim to avoid so called 'bad' emotions is the thing that makes the individual feel worse. Can you think of a time when you were feeling worried? Perhaps it was an exam, a presentation or seeing someone you hadn't seen for a long time... You may have then started to worry about being worried – 'why can't I be more confident? I shouldn't be feeling this way – I should be more positive'. The fight to avoid this emotion creates tension and additional stress.

Many of our young people experience this need to be 'happy' all of the time, which in turn can lead to increased masking (covered shortly). I remember working with a young man who had fallen over and was crying. I said to him "I can see you're sad" and he replied, sobbing, "I'm not sad, I'm a good boy!" Now, I was pretty sure his tear-stained face indicated that he was indeed, sad, but the narrative that had been taught from a young age was that good equals happy and bad equals sad. Our fairy tales reinforce this with the classic 'and they lived happily ever after' for the 'good guys', while the 'baddies' are grumbling miserably in a pit somewhere.

DOI: 10.4324/9781003350743-5

So you may be thinking that emotions are just tricky for everyone... and you'd be right! However, the extra challenges for autistic individuals may be that:

- It's trickier to identify these abstract concepts.

- Standard descriptions of emotions may not 'fit' the individual's experience.

- Communication of emotions may be different from neurotypicals.

- There are differences with interoception, meaning the individual has a different awareness of physiological (or inner body) states, which give us a hint about how we are feeling.

For around 50% of autistic individuals, there may also be uncertainty about the meaning of these physiological/bodily feelings (Gaigg et al., 2019). This is known as alexithymia: my heart is racing, but what does that mean?

So how do we support our neurodiverse young people to identify, communicate and respond to their emotions? There are a lot of tools being used to support autistic young people in schools across the world, but there is a lack of evidence to formally tell us what does and doesn't work. However, we know from accounts by parents and school staff, as well as initial publications such as the document *An evidence-based guide to anxiety in autism* by Sebastian Gaigg, Sarah Crawford and Helen Cottell (2019), that there are some things that are helping:

- Use of visual tools to make emotions more concrete and systematic.

- Role play of potentially uncertain situations in a safe environment (preparation in advance).

- Relaxation techniques tailored to the young person's sensory profile.

- Mindfulness activities such as focusing on the sensations in particular parts of the body, or on one sense at a time.

- Meditation activities such as noticing your thoughts but not engaging with them (avoiding that additional stress of 'worrying about worrying' that we looked at earlier).

- Individualised sensory activities.

- Activities that help unpick social interactions, such as drawing comic strips and labelling thoughts and feelings.

- Adapted Cognitive Behavioural Therapy (CBT).

- Increased predictability (visual schedules and sequences).

- Molehill Mountain App – Autistica have worked in partnership with King's College London to develop an app to help autistic people understand and self-manage anxiety. This is free to download from app stores.

Anxiety

It may not come as a surprise to hear that a high percentage of autistic individuals experience additional anxiety. In fact, while 10–15% of the general population will experience an anxiety disorder at some point in their lives, this is around 40% for autistic individuals (van Steensel et al., 2011).

Social interactions can be difficult to navigate and being able to focus intensely on one topic or thought (monotropic attention) can have its downsides.

"I can think about what I'm going to say in my head but bringing it out is really difficult. I need to think through my thoughts and the stress can put me off, so I have to work myself to that point of confidence. I like to think in advance but it's hard to prepare for how the other person might respond and if there are negative possibilities it puts me off.
At the end of the day, I will think about what I've done during the day and will cringe at any mistakes I've made, like causing an awkward situation or saying the wrong thing." – **Talhah**

"The other day, the teacher told me off for doing my work wrong. At break time I spoke to my friends about it. They didn't know why I was upset. They explained that she had just pointed out that I'd missed a question. She hadn't told me off. I can be really sensitive to things like that and worry about it for days." – **Fatima**

Coupling this intense analysis with the dismissive attitudes autistic individuals often face, goes some way to explain experiences of anxiety. In addition to this, as we have explored, extreme sensory input can feel overwhelming or even traumatic.

Then consider an environment that lacks routine, structure and a sense of control, and you can see how the combination of these factors can lead to feelings of anxiety.

Here Pavan shared some examples of scenarios that trigger anxiety as an autistic person:

- I am in the middle of something important and my phone goes off. I only have ten seconds to respond to it and I am not prepared, and I don't know what to expect. Panic and anxiety.

- It's the afternoon and I am tired after a busy day of school and I'm desperate to go back home but the bus stop is so crowded. I don't get on crowded buses, so I don't know how long until a less crowded bus turns up. Lots of anxiety due to uncertainty.

- I'm trying to finish a piece of schoolwork. It's due tomorrow. However, the work is not perfect enough. I want it to be perfect otherwise I will be disappointed and dissatisfied. However, it is getting late at night, but I still want to get it perfect.

- I have an appointment today. I prepare and set up for it. However, five minutes before the appointment, it is announced that it has been rescheduled. Frustration and anxiety due to a last-minute change.

- I am excited for a day trip outside. I'm prepared and ready to go. So much excitement! However, I arrive at the train station and there is an unexpected signal failure, so the trains are all cancelled. Disappointment, frustration and anxiety.

- I am in the middle of a task and whilst I'm doing that task, I have been asked to stop the task I am doing and to do something else. This makes me overwhelmed and anxious. I like to do things one by one.

- I am listening to someone speak and that person who is speaking says "look at me whilst I'm speaking" because I'm not maintaining eye contact. Very stressful. Additionally, my concentration is worse when I maintain eye contact.

- I go to the high street on Saturday afternoon, but someone is unexpectedly playing loud music on their trumpet. Oh dear. Very stressful.

- I'm trying to get to school but unexpectedly, there are roadworks so there is a huge traffic jam so I'm going to be late. So stressful. I hate being late.

- The fire alarm goes off unexpectedly so there has to be an evacuation causing a lot of panic. Not only is this unexpected, but it is also very loud. Unexpected change + loud noise = autistic meltdown.

- A person who I have never communicated with before approaches me and asks me for directions to the nearest supermarket. Lots of anxiety because I don't know that person and I have to communicate with them, and I can't just walk away.

Masking

In the young people's workbook, I explain this in detail, but I want to go through it here first with you as the adult facilitator. It is important to be aware of the difference between the typical behaviour of adapting to different contexts or scenarios (or what I have coined 'sunglassing'), and autistic 'masking'.

Everyone acts differently in different situations

friends

manager

We may act differently with our manager at work
compared to our friends at the weekend

Let's call this sunglassing

We may act in a way that makes us seem friendly,
hard-working or polite

When we do this, the rest
of our face is still on show

We are still our true selves and we can take the glasses off
whenever we want. We are not betraying our own sense of
identity.

You may be familiar with the description of a child 'holding it all together' in school, and then crumbling when they get home. In many cases, this is due to the pressure to 'conform' to be a certain way in society.

Masking or social camouflaging is the term used to describe this act of conforming. Think of it like putting on a mask to morph into the person you *think* you should be, or that others expect you to be.

"In class I try and sit at the back so I can watch what everyone else is doing. If they laugh at something, I laugh just a second behind everyone else. I just don't always know what they are laughing at." – **Fatima**

Many autistic people do something more than this, called masking

When you put on a mask, you hide your face, and people can't recognise who you are.

Autistic masking describes times when you behave in a certain way to get others to like you, or because you think this is what you should be doing.

It can be really tiring and damage self-esteem in the long term because you're not being your true self.

Many autistic people say they only take the 'mask' off when they are at home.

Masking can be accidentally encouraged:

Teacher says we must look at someone when they are speaking

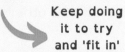

Force myself to give eye-contact even though I find it painful

Keep doing it to try and 'fit in'

Chapter 6

GIRLS

Did you know that more boys are currently diagnosed as being autistic than girls? However, this doesn't necessarily mean that boys are more likely to be autistic than girls. The diagnostic rate for girls has been steadily catching up. This, combined with research into this area, means that individuals now believe that boys and girls are equally likely to be autistic, it's just that fewer girls are diagnosed than boys (Loomes et al., 2017). In other words, lots of girls are being 'missed'. Why might this be? Well, there are lots of reasons for why the numbers might be different, including:

- Girls may be more likely to 'mask' or try to behave in a certain way to fit in (we will look at 'masking' in more detail later on).
- The process to identify autism has been set up to focus on the way autistic boys tend to behave.
- A lot of girls get diagnosed when they are grown up.

DOI: 10.4324/9781003350743-6

"I found out I was autistic when I was 11 years old, and I was over the moon because I knew I was different in the way I managed things compared to my friends and having a name for it helped me to understand what was causing my differences.

I knew I was different because I didn't like socialising as much as my friends did, I was very quiet, I also couldn't handle my emotions. When I got angry, I lashed out, and I was like 'this isn't what my peers do…' so I knew there must be something different.

I struggle with social situations – I'm great at making friends but maintaining friends and unwritten social rules I struggle with a lot.

My school were really helpful as they understood about my autism. I was able to go to a different quiet area for lunch and break times, so I didn't have to go outside. I was able to go to the canteen early so it wasn't so crowded. I also had an amazing SENCo who was always there for me.

It is so important to understand what the person's individual needs are and just accept them, for example, if they have sensory tools, letting them bring them to school discretely to use, or if they don't like to go outside, letting them stay inside at break and lunchtime. Just meeting their needs and also helping them understand they can manage.

It would help if people knew that if you've met one person with autism, you've met one person with autism. It's not always non-verbal boys who are autistic. This makes it very difficult for girls as there are still some people who say 'no it's just for boys'."
– **Thérèse**

We have touched on masking above, and it is important to remember that both males and females mask, this is not solely a female activity. There are also boys who present in a different way from the 'stereotypical' view of autism.

Historically, the concept of being autistic was developed based on observations and studies of groups of boys. This has meant that the diagnostic criteria, and understanding of autistic traits, has its foundations in male behaviour (Lai et al., 2015).

For example, people will sometimes say, "Oh they can't be autistic, they give eye contact!" This was a trait identified in initial studies related to boys, but really depends on the individual, and should not be an elimination criterion for assessment.

This is changing, and researchers and clinics are developing their diagnostic tools to ensure they recognise the ways that autistic individuals present, depending on their gender, culture and general personality.

Autism is like a colour-wheel

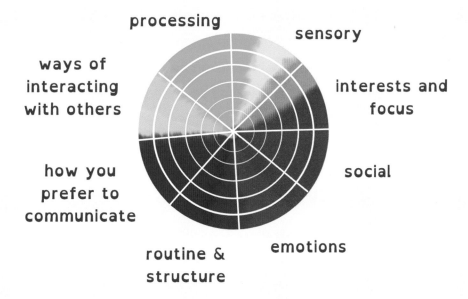

It can be helpful to think of autism as a bit like a colour wheel. There are lots of different combinations of colours, and each person's autistic identity will be unique to them.

"I was diagnosed at 32 years of age after two of my three daughters were diagnosed as being autistic. It was kind of after their diagnosis that I was able to get my diagnosis.

One of my daughters was diagnosed at 6 years of age, and one at 2, so being girls, we were very fortunate to have those early diagnoses. For autistic women, we know that in past generations and past decades, that just didn't happen. It's either that autism was seen as more of a male condition, or for those clinicians who were aware that autistic girls exist, they may not have had the right tools or clinical experience to spot us. That left us with a real fight on our hands to navigate the world.

It was really important for me to know I am autistic because life up until then was a complete confusion – I was just 'winging it'! And we all 'wing it', but by the time you're 27, you shouldn't be 'winging it' buying a pint of milk. You shouldn't have to be 'winging it' having a conversation with someone. You shouldn't have to be 'winging it' when you go out of an evening, in relationships and friendships and you're just improvising constantly. Imagine you've been to see a theatre show and you're sat at the back of the theatre, you're just there to have a nice time out. All of a sudden you get a tap on the shoulder, and you're led onto the stage. All of the actors around you have rehearsed this scene for months and you have no idea what's going to happen next. You don't know what you need to say, so you don't say anything and then people are annoyed at you. So, you just say something, anything, and you're constantly trying to get their reaction to see if you said the right thing. That's kind of how I felt and still do feel a lot of the time – like everyone else has got the script.

Our biggest vulnerability as autistic women is that we are hidden in plain sight a lot of the time. Often when I tell people I'm autistic, they say, "Oh, you don't look it!" – I don't know what that means! How am I supposed to 'look autistic'? I just say, well you haven't hung around long enough, because if you do, you will see the autistic behaviours, the autistic traits and the wonderful things being autistic can bring, as well as the huge challenges."

– Carly Jones MBE

I remember hearing about a lady in her 80s who had sought an autism assessment. Some people questioned the purpose, writing her off and wondering what the point was 'at her age'! Charming... In fact, this highlights the importance of understanding one's own identity. For this lady, she had lived most of her life feeling that she was different from the majority but wasn't sure why. She had questioned herself: Was she doing things wrong? Was she not clever enough? What was so 'wrong' with her that she struggled with things others seemed to find so simple? As time went on, she had shaped a life that worked for her, and yet she still had this niggling question in the back of her mind, asking what was different about her. For this woman, and many others, gaining a diagnosis of autism is a positive, affirming process. It explains your identity and gives permission to be proud of who you are. It also opens access to a community of people who share similarities with you. Each individual is different, and yet there's a shared understanding.

Chapter 7

DEBUNKING MYTHS

There are certain myths or stereotypes around autism that are unfortunately often still referred to. Previously there was a campaign from the National Autistic Society to try and increase 'awareness' of autism. The campaign concluded that the average 'man on the street' has heard of autism, but does not really understand it, and certainly doesn't understand the intricacies related to specific areas such as how gender comes into play.

Here are a few of the ones I regularly hear:

Must have an area of genius ability like 'Rainman'

- This misconception has come about because of the ability to delve deeper into areas of interest or hyperfocus (think back to the monotropism theory). However, the rate of savant syndrome (or being a certified genius) is the same as with the non-autistic population.

Everyone's a bit autistic!

- No, no, just no! I think people sometimes say this to try and empathise. However, it often has the opposite effect. Yes, there are traits that are part of an autism profile that are shared with people who aren't autistic. This is because they are human traits, and we are all human! However, the extent to which an autistic person experiences them, and the impact it has on their daily life, will be very different from someone who is not autistic. The only point to note here is that there are always undiagnosed autistic individuals who may be unaware of their autistic identity but share these traits.

DOI: 10.4324/9781003350743-7

Can't make eye contact

- While eye contact can be something autistic individuals find uncomfortable, or even painful, it is not an essential criterion for a diagnosis. Additionally, some individuals 'mask' throughout the day, and so will subject themselves to uncomfortable eye contact because they believe it is expected of them. I worked with an autistic teenage girl, sitting side by side to avoid too much eye contact, and her mum later told me that she had been practising eye contact all day before I came round. In the end she probably gave more eye contact than I did, but the point is, I was unaware this was something she found hard, because she masked her behaviour to hide this.

Sensory overload is 'just naughty behaviour'

- There is a clear difference between a tantrum and a meltdown or shutdown. There are lots of videos online of toddlers having tantrums. They drop to the floor flamboyantly and are observing and responding to the adult's reaction. If the adult moves away, they often follow. In contrast, when someone experiences sensory overload, they generally lose control and are unaware of the reactions of others. Just because you cannot see the trigger, doesn't mean it isn't real to that individual.

Can't be autistic as they are fine in school!

- Think back to the sections on masking and anxiety. This often explains those situations when someone behaves very differently from home to school. Remember, home is often the young person's safe place, where they feel accepted and comfortable enough to be their true self. You can also think of the day like a container. With each source of stress, a layer is poured into the container. As the day goes on, the layers build on one another and eventually, there is no room left, and the container overflows.

Stress Overflow

overwhelming smell

cover teacher

my lunch choice isn't available

someone asks for eye contact

train cancelled – I'm going to be late

loud noises

Don't care about others

- Various research projects led to the statement 'autistic people lack empathy' being banded around. While autistic individuals generally find social cues difficult to 'read', this does not mean they don't care about others. I worked with a child whose peer was upset and started crying. This young girl went up to her and stood very close, watching the tears roll down her face. Some people may interpret that as her 'lacking empathy' when in fact she was later able to explain that she found it difficult to understand what the other child was feeling and then felt so overpowered by her emotion that she didn't know how to respond.

Don't have a sense of humour

- This myth may have come about because autistic individuals may at times find different things funny from non-autistic people, and are less likely to engage in 'social laughter' – rather than just laughing at something that is genuinely funny. However, autistic people are just like non-autistic people – some people laugh more than others, and we all find different things funny.

Chapter 8

USING THE WORKBOOK

When to have these conversations?

This is a difficult question because I feel strongly that it's important for people to be aware of their autistic identity from as young an age as possible. However, there are factors that influence this:

• Cognitive understanding.

• Awareness of difference.

Children have different rates of cognitive development, and 'identity' is an abstract concept that can be challenging. Many children will start to notice differences between themselves and their peers and this often shows they are ready to have these discussions, but for some children, they won't ever talk about this.

Claire Sainsbury states "any child who is old enough to understand a simple explanation… is old enough" (Sainsbury, 2010, p. 126).

Likewise, research has found that when children know nothing about their diagnosis, they can have a very negative perception of themselves.

Things you want to try and avoid:

• Developing a negative understanding of autism (perhaps from societal narratives). Some young people hear the word 'autism', and it is used as a kind of insult, in a similar way that young people used to refer to people being 'so gay': 'you're so autistic'.

DOI: 10.4324/9781003350743-8

- Hearing about their autism identity accidentally (such as overhearing a conversation). I remember working with a family where the young boy knew something was going on because his older sister had been listening in to parent's conversations. This led to her telling him he had something major wrong with him and was probably going to die. Not a great starting point for a positive discussion around difference...

Who is best placed to deliver the sessions?

> *"When you are autistic, sometimes you feel like a leaf in a cul-de-sac blowing round in circles. It feels like you're not going anywhere, and no one understands you. Then one day, someone picks you up and realises you can go somewhere else – someone understands you."* **– Willard Wigan MBE**

Your feelings

If you are the young person's parents or carers, it is likely that you will have your own thoughts and feelings about this whole process. You may have battled for years to try and get an autism assessment or are carrying the weight of comments from 'well-meaning' family members or professionals. There may be layers of guilt or worry that you are doing the best for your child. I have worked with many, many families over the years and I can tell you, that is all 'normal', whatever that means!

If you are a professional, I expect you have one eye on your never-ending 'to-do' list and another on this book. I've worked in education for 15 years so trust me, I get it!

However, for this process to be as positive as possible for your young person, it is **really** important that you are in a calm place emotionally and can give the individual your all during these sessions. Parents, if you're worried you might get upset, practise talking through the book beforehand. Highlight sections you want to remember, or dare I say it, try a little role play with an understanding companion (yes, I'm still talking about the book!)...

Alternatively, consider if you are the best person to start this conversation. You may feel that you **should** because of your role, but as I've mentioned, this is a lifelong journey, so there is plenty of time for you to be involved. It isn't a 'cop out' to pass this over to another family member, or someone from school. It's not a reflection on your skills as a parent. Remember, our emotions often are contagious - if we are feeling highly anxious, those around us may well mirror these feelings or behaviours. Always consider whose needs you are meeting – if you are doing this because you feel you need to, but it's not in the best interests of your child, it might be best to let someone else take the lead, while you access support and develop your own understanding of autism.

It is important that the lead adult is able to keep calm, give enough processing time and speak about autism very positively.

Parents/carers

If you are the young person's parent/carer, and you are not feeling emotionally ready to have the initial conversation with your child, you can ask if there is someone available at school to go through the book, and then you could come in for the final session. It would be very confusing for your child if they are being told that autism is a positive part of their identity, but you are getting very upset during the sessions. Likewise, you may feel that you are the closest parent/carer to the child, but it may be better for your partner to lead these sessions, because they have a calmer, more patient temperament. This is not a competition! Don't lay any guilt on yourself, there will be plenty of time to have lots of great positive conversations about their autistic identity. This is the start of the journey – but it is very important that it's a positive start.

School

As above with parents/carers, it may not be the person that works with them the most. The key features of the person are:

- A positive understanding of autism.
- Being willing to be accommodative of the autistic person.
- A positive approach to difference.
- A calm, patient manner.

If you have a staff member who is more confident in leading these sessions, but does not know the young person well, you could do a joint session. Likewise, if the young person is anxious about going to these sessions with a new person, a familiar staff member could attend alongside the young person. It is important to agree their role in advance, to ensure that the person leading is still in control.

The chosen adult

The role of the chosen adult should be:

- To be a reassuring presence (with minimal verbal input).

- To support with processing (providing additional visual tools or methods that work for that young person).

- To provide examples to help the young person identify with the features discussed.

In advance of the session, you should start planning and information gathering alongside parents. There is an 'Information Gathering' sheet available in the resources section which can be used in an informal meeting with parents/carers and key adults.

Working as a team around the child: School

If you have identified a need for the young person to understand their diagnosis, it is vitally important that parents/carers are onboard. It is key for young people to understand their autism identity from as early as possible for them to process it, but if this happens at a time when parents/carers are not emotionally able to support and ensure this is a positive experience, it could have longer term negative consequences. If parents/carers are not yet ready, focus on signposting them to resources to help them develop their own understanding.

If parents/carers are happy for this process to go ahead, it is vital that you communicate regularly with them:

- Ahead of the sessions to find out what the child's starting point is (do they have any understanding of autism, and if so, what words do they use?)

- To find out if there are any timetabling points to be aware of (see below).

- After each session so they are aware of what you have covered and any possible questions that may come up (plus how to respond).

- After each session sharing the feedback comments from the young person on what they have learnt.

Ensure you are open with the young person about communication with home, so that they know that everyone is on the same page.

Working as a team around the child: Parents/carers

If you are working through this book at home, you may well want to share the completed version, or elements of it, with the school. There are sections such as the personal passport that can help the team around the young person to understand them better. This is also usually empowering for the young person, so they don't feel that they have this new 'secret' at home that no one in school is aware of.

Planning the sessions

To ensure this process is as empowering and positive as possible, it is a good idea to spend some time information-gathering before you start.

In school

I have previously delivered sessions where the young person is taken out of class and missed their favourite lesson, so not only were we starting off on the back foot, but they were so anxious about missing this lesson that they couldn't focus on anything we were doing.

Another time, I had a session with a boy who was highly anxious. At the end of the session, he told me that the room we were in was usually used as a 'time out' sanction area, for those who had misbehaved at lunchtime. He was worried the whole time that he was in 'trouble'.

On a separate occasion, we were in a room with the electricity switchboard for the whole school up on the wall, buzzing away. Another time, we were next to the hall where a whole year group were singing at the top of their lungs. Now, I'm fully aware there's usually a lack of 'spare' space available in schools, but it does pay to spend a little time considering what would work best for this young person, even if that's somewhere slightly unconventional.

Here are some things to consider:

- How long should the sessions be? Depending on the age and attention span, you probably want to aim for each session to be 20–60 minutes, which would include time to check in and do something they are passionate about at the end (you'll find example structures throughout the book).

- Where? Ideally a familiar place or somewhere they feel comfortable. This doesn't have to be indoors – they may prefer to be outside but do consider distractions and external noise.

- Consider seating: for example, would they prefer to be sitting side by side at a table, lying on the floor, sitting on bean bags or on a wobble cushion?

- No interruptions: have a 'busy' sign on the door or pull the blinds down. Think of this like a therapy session. If you were going to see a therapist in your place of work, would you want your colleagues walking past peering in, or popping in to do some photocopying while you were unpicking key aspects of your identity? I think not…

As school staff, you may not know the full 'ins and outs' of the young person's schedule and preferences. It would be worth scheduling a meeting with the parents/carers to find out:

- What lessons they can miss (from both parent/carer's perspective of what they are happy for the child to miss and from the young person's point of view in terms of lessons they enjoy or would feel anxious about missing).

- Is there a day of the week to avoid? Perhaps they always go to bed slightly later on a Wednesday and so Thursdays aren't a good idea…

- What about time of day? Are they more attentive in the morning, or more relaxed and receptive at the end of the day?

At home/outside of school

If you are a family member or another professional planning on delivering sessions outside of school, similar principles apply as above.

- How long should the sessions be? Depending on the age and attention span, you probably want to aim for each session to be 20–60 minutes, which would include time to check in and do something they are passionate about at the end (you'll find example structures throughout the book).

- Where? This is slightly trickier at home as it depends on what your home routines are. If the young person has a set place for work, they may like to sit there, or it may feel too much like homework. Similarly, they may prefer to lie under the kitchen table, or in bed, so that they can relax and feel comfortable. Likewise, it may be that the house isn't the best place. Perhaps it would feel more like a treat for them if you went out to the local park for a picnic or went and sat in Grandma's garden. You know your child best and will know where they will be able to concentrate enough to take in these new concepts in a relaxed way.

- Time of day: parents often ask me why all the questions come out at bedtime, and this is often because this is the time when the young person truly processes the day. With this in mind, it's a good idea to consider how close to bedtime you are having these sessions, as they could be overloaded with new information, which could impact their sleep. A weekend late morning or early afternoon would probably be a good time.

- Consider seating – for example, would they prefer to be sitting side by side at a table, lying on the floor, sitting on bean bags, or having their dog next to them to stroke while they are talking?

- No interruptions – if you have other people in your household, consider how you can keep them amused (or removed!) during this time. Your young person will be able to concentrate more easily without additional distractions, and you will also feel more relaxed if you are only focusing on one thing at once. Your young person may want to share some or all of their completed book with siblings or other family members at the end, but this is their choice, and this initial stage is personal to them.

Key strategies for using the workbook

> *"I don't like blending in, being like everyone else to me is very boring. I want to be someone who is different. Just being like everyone else sounds like the most boring thing in the world to me."* – **Ali**

Choose the right time: if the young person is absorbed in their interests, or fixated on something that has happened, it may not be the right time. Leave it until they are able to focus on and process the information.

Allow processing time: don't talk 'at' the young person, leave silent space. If you struggle with this, try counting to 10 or 20 in your head while you wait.

Don't talk too much: try to keep language concise.

Use the young person's name to cue them in: they may be focusing on something else.

Sit side by side: ever found those difficult conversations flow much better when in the car or on a walk? It is a lot easier to listen, process and respond when you aren't sitting face to face. Where possible consider sitting side by side. If this isn't possible, try not to give too much eye contact as this adds another layer of input for the young person to process and can detract from their overall understanding of the topic.

Consider the environment: how can you make the space more appealing to their sensory needs?

- Would it be better to have low lighting, rather than the bright strip lights?

- Can you provide fidget tools to help aid concentration and sensory regulation? Even the humble blu-tack is a great one!

- Is there a certain scent they love – could you have a tissue with lavender drops on to create a sensory place of peace?

- Can you have other sensory tools available such as a weighted blanket or wobble cushion?

Use visuals to support complex concepts: have scraps of paper, note cards or a mini-whiteboard on hand to draw something visually to help support your explanations. For example, in the sensory section, you may want to draw out the zig zag lines in front of the young person, to help them understand sensory sensitivity:

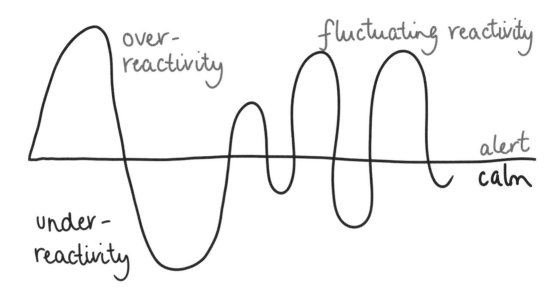

Use specialist interests to engage your child/young person in the topics.

Have a plan for follow up questions: we've all been there – with time and energy to face the complex questions, but they don't come until you're making dinner/dismissing them at the end of the day, and suddenly they drop the question of all questions, and you're unprepared!

It's OK to 'park' the question or give the young person a kind of 'holding message' – better this than to give a rushed answer that they later find confusing or unsettling.

One way of doing this can be to record the question visually and have an allocated time to come back to it. You can do this with:

- A mini whiteboard.

- A stack of post it notes.

- A special notepad.

- A questions box.

- An email chain.

- Voice notes.

The understanding is that the young person (independently, or with support) can record the questions they have (through drawings or written language), and you will agree on a set time when you will come together and go through them. For the young person, it can also be useful knowing that they have protected time to explore this further, and they don't need to process everything on the spot.

Language and approaches

> *"Just because you can't see something, doesn't mean it doesn't exist; just because you can't see an ability in someone doesn't mean it's not there. It's like a box. Open up the lid, find it, show them, encourage them – it blossoms."* – **Willard Wigan MBE**

The aim of these sessions is to develop a positive sense of self, and so the language used throughout these conversations must have an inclusive focus.

There are certain terms or phrases that will threaten this process and should be avoided.

Things not to say

- ASD or autism spectrum disorder.
- 'Normal'.
- Severe/mild.
- High/low functioning.

> *"I prefer to say 'autism' and not 'ASD'. 'ASD' stands for 'autistic spectrum disorder'; the use of the word 'disorder' has negative connotations. It is very important to realise that autism is NOT negative."* – **Pavan**

Big 'buts' vs the simple 'and'

- The word 'but' is one to avoid when trying to convey a positive message. Think of a time when your boss/partner/friend said to you, "You've done a really good job there, but I need you to do these other things as well." Generally, people immediately focus on what is lacking, and leave the interaction with a negatively weighted message.

- As soon as you hear the word 'but', any positives before the 'but' are dismissed or forgotten, e.g., "Being autistic means you're good at certain things, but you find other things trickier."

- Instead replace the 'but' with a simple 'and'. 'And' allows two facts to join together, rather than one challenging the meaning of the other.

Things not to do

- Do not insist on eye contact (this can be painful for some and for others it can hinder their ability to process what you are saying/reading).

- Do not rush the young person – it should be a calm environment where they feel valued.

- Do not put words into their mouth – wait for them to explain things, don't jump in.

- Do not communicate too much information in a short space of time – it could cause sensory overwhelm.

Understanding your own identity is vital to develop a positive understanding of self, and in the long term, boost wellbeing.

Structuring the sessions

First and most important message… do not complete in one sitting!

This is a process. The journey of understanding your own identity is ongoing and so we want to break up the steps into small, digestible chunks, so the young person has time to understand, reflect and potentially ask any questions before you move onto the next chunk.

An example of how you could structure it could be:

Session 1 (45 mins–1 hour)	Introduction My physical identity My personality Feeling different
Session 2 (1 hour)	What autism is My autism identity: Interests and focus
Session 3 (1 hour)	My autism identity: Social and communication
Session 4 (1 hour +)	My autism identity: Sensory
Session 5 (1 hour)	My autism identity: Routine and structure My autism identity: Masking and stimming My autism identity: Emotions and energy levels
Session 6 (1 hour +)	Other autistic individuals My toolkit My personal passport My autism identity statement Self-advocacy

- Some sections will take longer than others depending on how responsive the young person is – you may find the more you do, the longer they take!

- Go with the flow – if they are opening up and talking freely, and you are going over the allocated time slot but are able to continue, I would suggest you do so, until it comes to a natural pause point.

- Try to end each session at a clear point (even if not the end of that section), so that the young person doesn't feel abandoned halfway through a new concept.

- For young people who need additional processing time, you may want to double the number of sessions, but cover less in each one.

- Have a look at the section on 'Other autistic individuals'. Would your young person prefer to look at the 11 profiles all in one go, as proposed above, or would they prefer to look at one or two at the end of each session?

- Always find time for something fun/reflective at the end of the session. Not only does this ease the transition back to their usual routine, but it also ends on a positive note, which may help their overall processing of the topic. Examples of these could be:

○ A game they enjoy (a physical game or on an electronic device).

○ A visit to their favourite place, e.g., the vegetable patch in school, or a walk to the park outside of school.

○ A sensory-based game that is only used at the end of the session.

○ Their favourite YouTube video.

○ Time to talk about one of their passions, e.g., you could ask them to tell you three things about roller coasters.

○ Sharing photos of their favourite things, or something they did at the weekend.

○ Mindfulness activities, e.g., YouTube guided meditations or mindful colouring.

At the start of every session, write out a plan. This can be on a mini-whiteboard, on your phone or a post-it note or scrap of paper. Share this with the young person and empower them to check back to the schedule to keep you both on track. (I often find the schedule is a useful tool for me as the supporting adult as well.) They may want to cross items off as you complete them or put a tick next to them. Use whatever language works best for your young person: plan, timetable, schedule etc.

In the example below, the young person was a big Lego fan, so this is what we used as the fun activity for the last five minutes of the session (I will use Lego in the examples throughout the session guidance notes, but please adapt based on your young person's interests).

Our Plan:

1. Title + contents page
2. Introduction
3. My physical identity
4. My personality and interests
5. Likes and dislikes
6. Personality traits
7. Feeling different
8. The Neurodiversity Pencil Case
9. Recap and rating
10. Lego
11. Back to class / lunch

Recap and rating

At the end of each session, it is useful to give a very brief recap of the topics covered, to help with processing. Then, you can ask the young person these simple questions to gain their insights into the session, and to ensure they feel valued and empowered in this process:

1. What did you like about the session?

2. What did you learn?

3. What would make it better?

If you are completing sessions in school and want to keep a record of this feedback, you could create a simple online form.

Whether in home, or at school, ensure you act on the feedback wherever possible. For example, in one of my sessions, a young person told me they were more able to concentrate when they are sketching while talking, so the next week we arranged for them to bring in their sketchbook for our session. Likewise, you may discover strategies that would be useful to use in class.

If sessions are taking place in school, this feedback from the young person is valuable to share with parents/carers, to ensure they are involved and can continue the conversation at home.

Chapter 9

SECTION GUIDANCE

This next section contains guidance notes and prompts for the example structure shared previously. You have the freedom to structure the sessions in a way that works for the young person and your day. Do remember that these timings are just a guide, and it could take more or less time.

Guidance relates to the sections in the book, but the example visual schedules match the example structure shared previously. If you plan to cover more or fewer sections in your session, just amend the schedule accordingly.

Where there are sections of text in the young person's workbook, check if they would like to read in their head, read aloud, or for you to read for them. Likewise, when there are opportunities for writing, check if they would like to write, or prefer you to write for them. Keep checking each session – their preferences may change.

DOI: 10.4324/9781003350743-9

SESSION 1

Introduction
My physical identity
My personality and interests
Feeling different

Visual schedule:

1. Title and contents page
2. Introduction
3. My physical identity - fingerprints
4. My personality and interests
5. Likes and dislikes
6. Personality traits
7. Feeling different
8. The Neurodiversity Pencil Case
9. Recap and rating
10. Positive activity, e.g., Lego
11. Back to class/home activity

Our Plan:

1. Title + contents page
2. Introduction
3. My physical identity
4. My personality and interests
5. Likes and dislikes
6. Personality traits
7. Feeling different
8. The Neurodiversity Pencil Case
9. Recap and rating
10. Lego
11. Back to class / lunch

Key messages

- The aim of this book is to better help you understand your own identity.

- This is a positive experience.

- Take your time – we will do little bits at a time.

- This book is a resource for you to keep coming back to.

- We all have different physical identities, likes, dislikes, personality traits and ways of perceiving the world.

- In teams, we need all different types of people and ways of thinking.

- Our brains all work in different ways – we all interact with the world, think, learn, and experience the world differently.

DOI: 10.4324/9781003350743-10

Things to remember

- Leave thinking time. If you ask a question and they say 'not sure' or deflect it, it may be that they need some time to process the question. Just wait and count to 10. You could then repeat the question, and refer to the visual supports.

- Have a range of fidget tools available and remind the young person that they are all there for them to use (you could also discretely model using them so they can see these are tools that lots of people use).

Resources

- Fidget tools.

Common questions/comments

Why do we need to do this?	The same as you learn about people in school like Mary Seacole and Florence Nightingale, it's important to learn more about yourself. This book will help you to know yourself better.
How will that help me?	Learning more about yourself means you can understand what you need and ask for it, perhaps in school or when you are older.
I read that fingerprints aren't actually all different...	It's true that people can share the same number of arches, loops, and whorls on their fingers, but they will still have different configurations of minutiae - perhaps one to research later!

Possible prompts

Go through the workbook, following the order given. Remember to tick off each point on the schedule as you go through. Below are a few guidance points.

Title page

Either leave the young person to complete independently, or you can give the following prompts:

- Gender identity: how they see themselves in terms of gender (this may correlate with their assigned sex at birth or may differ). It's important this book acknowledges their identity as a whole.

- Ethnicity: this should be how the young person perceives themselves and may differ from the ethnicity of their parents. For example, parents may define themselves as Asian, while the young person sees themselves as Asian British. This is an

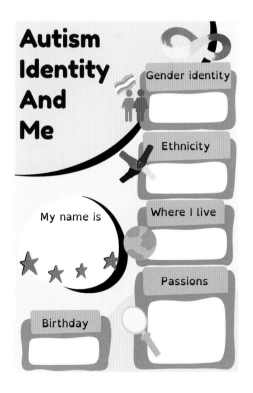

important area to include as it will feature on forms related to 'identity' throughout their lives.

- Where I live: location as defined by the young person – can be country, county, town, or even postal address.

- Passions: areas of intense interest or specialist knowledge. These will be referred to later on when exploring autistic traits.

My physical identity

- Compare the two drawings and discuss similarities and differences. Note that although clothes aren't 'physical features', the clothes people choose to wear can be a way of expressing their identity and may change in different situations.

- Similar – both have brown eyes.

- Differences – hair colour, height, shoe size and other features.

- Here is a blank copy for you to complete at the same time as the young person:

Eyes:

Hair:

Other features:

Height:

Shoe size:

Favourite clothes:

Copyright material from Duffus (2023), *Autism, Identity and Me*, Routledge

- Now compare your physical appearance with your young person's – what looks the same and what is different?

My personality and interests

- Below is a blank copy for you to complete at the same time as your young person. You can then compare your likes and dislikes.

- While filling it out you can give prompts related to the ones you are selecting, e.g., I'm going to think about foods I like and don't like...

- Ideas of prompts to consider: food, subjects/lessons, habits, places, animals, things to do, colours, books, films, seasons etc.

Likes

Dislikes

Copyright material from Duffus (2023), *Autism, Identity and Me*, Routledge

Personality traits

- If there are any words that the young person may struggle to understand, help to explain them.

- Here is a copy for you to complete and then compare your answers:

Calm	**Curious**	**Energetic**
Hardworking	**Playful**	**Friendly**

Honest

Caring

Serious

Sense of humour

Optimistic

Daring

Sensitive

Imaginative

Talkative

Now draw any others that describe you:

- Go through their choices and reinforce positives, for example, 'yes, you do have a good sense of humour'.

Feeling different

- Option to draw a chart here to get the young person to compare them:

Same	Different
Both fruit	Different colour
Both round	Different texture
Both have seeds inside	Different taste

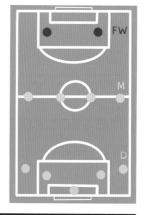

Team roles

- Highlight the different roles in the image: FW=forward, M=midfielder, D=defender

Example forward/defender table below:

Forward	Defender
Attackers go forward with the ball	Defenders stay back
Attack the opposing goal	Defend their goal

- Highlight that those two positions are quite different, but you need them both in a team to make them work well.

Neurodiversity

- Discuss with the young person – have they heard of it before?

- What do they think it means?

- Neuro = brains or nervous system. Diverse = different. So, neurodiversity = different brains.

Did you know...

- Just like our physical identity, likes/dislikes and personality, our brains are all different too.

Neurodiversity

∞

neurotypical
brains processing in the way most people do

neurodivergent
brains processing in a different, equally good, way

- That word, neurodiversity, describes the differences of all the brains in the world. Neurotypical describes someone whose brain processes in the way most people do. You would describe yourself as neurodivergent, as you process information in a different, equally good, way.

- Discuss the quote: What do you think of that? Do you like to blend in or be different?

- The boy who said that was 13 – sometimes it gets easier to feel confident being different, the older you get.

The Neurodiversity Pencil Case

Pens/pencils comparison table prompts:

- Tell me what pens are really good at?

- What lessons would you use pens/pencils for?

Differences could include:

Positive things about pens	Positive things about pencils
• Better if you don't want someone to be able to rub it out • Good if you are writing something important	• Better for drawing • You can rub them out

- Just briefly introduce the term autism and explain you will be exploring this further in future sessions.

- You may want to record their understanding of autism on a separate sheet of paper.

- You can then come back to this at the end of the sessions to show the progress they have made in understanding this concept.

- Do not write it in their book, as they may be starting out with negative connotations of autism, and we do not want these to be ingrained in their book.

Recap and rating

Share next week's topic: 'What autism is' and 'My autism identity: Interests and focus'.

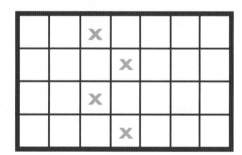

Before we play Lego/name activity, can you tell me:

- What did you like about the session?

- What did you learn?

- What would make it better?

If appropriate, discuss the questions above and explain when you will have the next session. If possible, show these visually on a calendar, or send calendar invites.

Engage in the positive activity together to complete the session.

SESSION 2

What autism is
My autistic identity: Interests and focus

Visual schedule:

1. Check in
2. What autism is
3. Girls and boys
4. The Neurodiversity Orchestra
5. My autistic identity: Interests and focus
6. Recap and rating
7. Positive activity, e.g., Lego
8. Back to class/home activity

Our Plan:
1. Check in
2. What autism is
3. Girls and boys
4. The Neurodiversity Orchestra
5. My autistic identity:
   — interests and focus
6. Recap and Rating
7. lego
8. Back to class / lunch

Key messages

- Being autistic means I am part of a shared identity.

- I am not the only person who is autistic.

- Autism will not hurt me, and it won't go away - it's part of my identity.

- Autism is a different way of perceiving the world.

- You have your own unique autistic identity.

DOI: 10.4324/9781003350743-11

Resources

- Fidget tools.

- Set of 17 pencils and 4 pens (different colours and styles if possible). If you don't have this amount, just make sure you have more pencils than pens.

- Red/green cards.

- Adult should read advice section before 'My autistic identity' in advance.

Common questions/comments

Why didn't anyone tell me before (that I'm autistic)?	Identity is a complicated concept and it's difficult to understand when you're very young.
	It's also really important that you understand this part of your identity in a positive way and so we didn't want to rush these conversations. We wanted to talk about it when we all have time.
I know someone who's autistic and they don't speak at all - will I stop speaking?	Autism is like a constellation or colour wheel - you share similarities with other autistic people, but your autistic identity is different from theirs.
I thought autism meant you are not very good at things?	As with everyone, there are some things you are good at, and others you find trickier.
	If you are able to, you can work on the things you find trickier, but it's important for you to find the things you are good at and focus on these.

Possible prompts
Check in

- Use a visual emotion check-in tool here, such as the basic EmEn Check-in (which we will cover in more detail later in the book) so the young person can share how they are feeling.

- Recap the last session (we all have different physical identities, likes, dislikes, personality traits and ways of perceiving the world).

What autism is

- Point out the formation of stars on the colour wheel and that each star relates to a trait.

- Highlight the stars in different places in the two images.

The Neurodiversity Orchestra

- Look at the table together and discuss their understanding or experience of any of these instruments.

- Notice how they are played in slightly different ways.

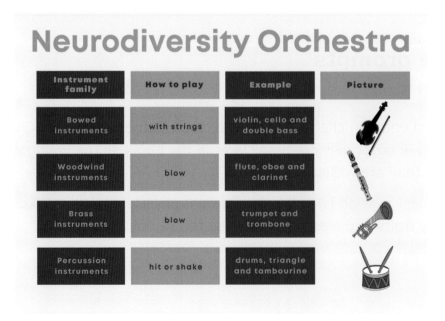

- Relate this to them: What role do you think you're best at? Can you think of other people who are good at the other roles?

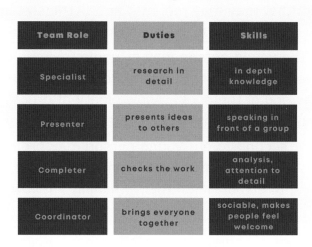

Neurodiversity Orchestra

Team Role	Duties	Skills
Specialist	research in detail	in depth knowledge
Presenter	presents ideas to others	speaking in front of a group
Completer	checks the work	analysis, attention to detail
Coordinator	brings everyone together	sociable, makes people feel welcome

My autistic identity:

Autistic identity traits guidance

Read this to yourself before you start this section:

- In this section it is vitally important that the young person's voice is recorded, word for word (or as close to as possible).

- At the start, establish whether the young person would like you to write for them in this section, or whether they would like to write themselves. Even if they are confident writers, it is generally easier if someone else records their words here as they can then just focus on their thoughts and reflections, and you can ensure it is written down.

- For each example trait/picture, you could:
  - Read the **statement in your guidance notes.**
  - Read the **quotes in the workbook.**
  - Ask 'Does this sound like you?'
  - Wait.
  - Record answer (if they want you to).

- With each picture it is important to give the young person processing time. **Read the relevant sections and then wait.**

- If you are struggling with the silence, you can count to 10–20 in your own head, to give them plenty of time to process.

- If they do not respond, you could read the statement again, in exactly the same words. Changing the wording means they have more words to process.
- If you feel that they don't relate to the statement but aren't sure what to do, remind them that they may feel that not all the statements apply to them, and they can say "No" or "this isn't me".
- If you feel that the young person may struggle to communicate this verbally, have red and green cards ready to support with this (see Resources at the end of the book). Allow plenty of processing time, as before, and then prompt them to point to a card to choose.
- As with the other sections, your young person may prefer to read the quotes to themselves and may want to comment on the pictures without you even needing to elaborate on their meaning – follow their lead.

Key points:

- These are examples of some characteristics that autistic people experience.
- It's OK if they don't all apply to your young person.
- Take your time to include lots of their own examples to make sure it's personalised.

Interests and focus

- Introduce the theory. You may want to use this wording: Some people have 'monotropic attention' and others have 'polytropic attention'.
- Try to relate the example to their interests.

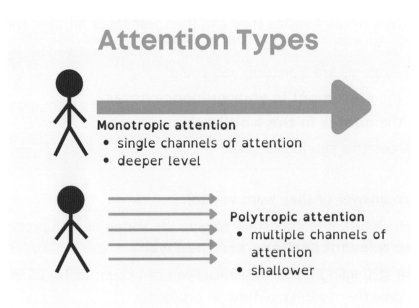

Example wording for traits

Focus/attention

Focus/attention

- This theory explains why some autistic people find that they are able to focus their attention on something that they are interested in for long periods of time. They might not notice other things happening around them.

- Some people might describe this as having a good 'attention to detail'. You may be able to notice things that other people aren't aware of.

Amazing imagination

Amazing imagination

- Some autistic people have an amazing imagination. You may be able to create worlds or stories in your head that other people can't.

Expert in my interests

Expert in my interests

- Some autistic people spend a lot of time on their interests or passions. They can become experts in their area of interest as they know so much about that topic. It could be anything, from the names of dinosaurs, to London transport routes, information about a certain celebrity or how lampposts work.

The 3 Ps

- The 3 Ps describe different types of interests: passions, phases, and pastimes. A passion is something that is an ongoing specialist interest (sometimes shortened to SpIn by the autistic community). This is something you feel passionately about and the interest has lasted for a long period of time. What are your passions?

the 3 Ps

passion — an ongoing area of interest, sometimes called a SpIn (special interest)

phase — a short-term interest, may also be a SpIn but just for one period of your life

pastime — something you do regularly for enjoyment

- A phase is a short-term interest, which may also be a SpIn, but for a shorter period of time – perhaps something you were passionate about when you were younger, but aren't anymore. Can you think of any for you?

- A pastime is something that you enjoy doing, but you don't feel so strongly about. It could be a type of exercise, a series you watch or something you read about. Can you think of any pastimes?

Switching attention

- Some autistic people find it tricky to shift attention from one thing to another. For example, if the teacher asks you to stop what you are writing and look at the board, this could be hard. You have to stop what you are writing midway through a task (when you might not be finished) and then move your eyes from looking at your page, up to looking at the board.

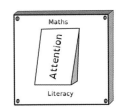

Switching attention

Different interests

- Some autistic people find that their interests, or passions, are different from other people their age.

- Here it is important to highlight that girls may have similar interests to their peers, but the intensity of this interest may be to a deeper level, e.g., interested in makeup, but spend two hours doing it every morning.

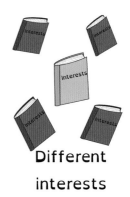

Different interests

Organisation

- Some autistic people find it tricky to remember things, particularly at school when there are more things to remember, e.g., homework, sports kits, lunch etc.

- Some autistic people like to have systems to help them keep organised.

Organisation

Amazing memory for certain things

- Some autistic people have really good memories for things they are interested in. It could be things they read about a long time ago.

Amazing memory
for
certain things

Imagining in pictures

- This is like the amazing imagination – many autistic people find it easier to process visual information, or pictures, than lots of spoken words.

- You could also prompt the young person to reflect on their ways of thinking – do they usually 'see' still or moving images when they think, or do they 'hear' their thoughts?

Imagining
in pictures

Recap and rating

Share next week's topic: 'My autistic identity: Social and communication'.

Before we play Lego/name activity, can you tell me:

- What did you like about the session?

- What did you learn?

- What would make it better?

If appropriate, discuss the questions above and explain when you will have the next session.

Engage in the positive activity together to complete the session.

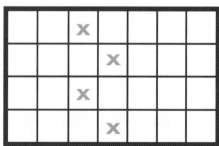

SESSION 3

My autistic identity: Social and communication

Visual schedule:

1. Check in
2. Social
3. Communication
4. My communication identity
5. Recap and rating
6. Positive activity, e.g., Lego
7. Back to class/home activity

Our Plan:

1. Check in
2. Social
3. Communication
4. My communication identity
5. Recap and rating
6. Lego
7. Back to class/ lunch

Key messages

• Autistic individuals can find it tricky in social situations.

• It can be easier when communicating with other neurotypical people, or people that you feel understand you and your preferences.

• There aren't any right or wrong ways of communicating.

• It's useful to know your communication identity, as you can share this with others who may expect you to communicate in what they see as 'typical' ways.

Resources

• Fidget tools.

• Red/green cards.

DOI: 10.4324/9781003350743-12

Common questions/comments

If I'm neurodivergent doesn't that just mean I'm 'weird'?	Definitely not! Just look up famous neurodivergent people and you will find many scientists, artists, inventors and singers who are neurodivergent – at least 1 in 7 people are!
I don't feel like anyone wants to be my friend.	What do you like doing at break times? Perhaps we could set up a neurodivergent group that focuses on one of your passions/interests? Meeting people who share your interests/similarities is a good starting point for building friendships.

Possible prompts
Check in

- Use a visual emotion check-in tool here, such as the basic EmEn Check-in (which we will cover in more detail later in the book) so the young person can share how they are feeling.

- Recap the last session (what autism is and their autism identity: interests and focus).

You may want to refer back to the 'Autistic identity traits guidance' section from Session 2 before you start this section.

Example wording for social traits

Talking to new people

- Some autistic people find it very stressful when they have to talk to new people. This could be when joining a new school, meeting new teachers, buying something in a shop, ordering something in a restaurant or talking to family friends. It can be hard to know what to say and how to start the conversation.

Talking to
new people

Working alone

- Some autistic people prefer to work on their own as they know what to expect and it is more predictable than working in a group. It can be tricky when doing group projects at school, e.g., in science, or having to talk to your partner and not knowing what to say.

- Some people find it easier to work with other neurodivergent people, or those that they feel understand them better.

Busy places

- Some autistic people find it can be difficult to be in places where there are lots of other people, like the school hall, train stations, airports, cinema, restaurants and shopping centres. Lots of people usually means it is noisy and unpredictable.

Listening to the teacher

- Some autistic people find it's tricky to listen to someone who is doing lots of talking, and there isn't anything visual to look at to help process the information. This links back to the one last time on 'imagining in pictures'. Autistic people tend to be really good at processing visual/picture information but find it harder if it's all just speaking.

Playing with others

- Some autistic people find it tricky playing games where the rules change, like playground football. Some people feel left out of games or don't know what to do. Some people also find it hard when they lose games. Some people find it easier to play with other neurodivergent individuals, or those who understand their preferences.

- Some autistic people may find it hard to make friends (or find a 'best friend') or might focus all their energy on one person.

- It might be easier to interact with people who are older or younger, rather than the same age – may be described as very 'mature'.

Communication

- You could discuss idioms/metaphors/sarcasm here and see if they have examples of when they have found these tricky to understand the underlying meaning.

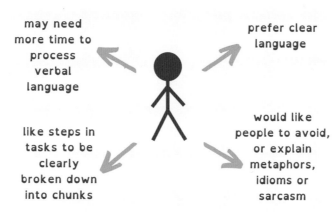

may need more time to process verbal language

prefer clear language

like steps in tasks to be clearly broken down into chunks

would like people to avoid, or explain metaphors, idioms or sarcasm

autistic communication styles

Ways of showing you care

- Can you think of a time someone has done one of these things for you?

- Can you think of a time someone has wanted you to do one of these things and you haven't wanted to? An example here may be being told to hug a family member when the young person doesn't want to – this would be a good opportunity to discuss boundaries and consent around bodies and touch.

giving your full attention

doing something together

helping them

hugs and kisses

asking about their day

gifts

compliments

holding hands

putting notes in their lunchbox

telling someone you love them

typical ways of showing you care

My communication identity

Example text to describe Pavan's communication identity:

- Pavan is quiet when he meets new people, he finds it hard to start a conversation, even though he can be quite chatty once he gets going.

- He doesn't bother with small talk, like 'how was your weekend', or talking about the weather.

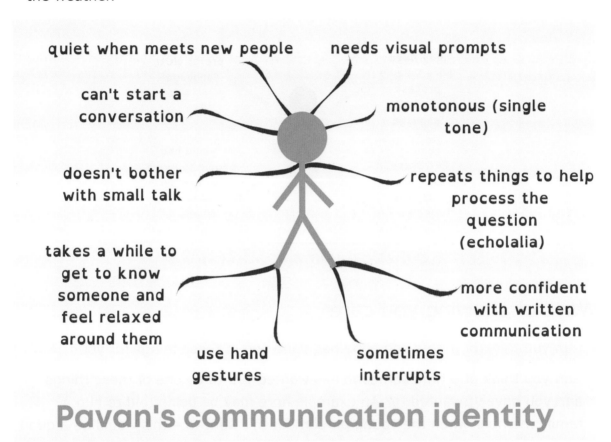

- It takes Pavan a while to get to know someone and feel relaxed around them.

- He uses lots of hand gestures to get his points across and sometimes he interrupts because he has really important things in his brain that he wants to share.

- He is more confident writing emails than speaking and he repeats things to help him process the question (echolalia).

- He also speaks in a monotonous tone and likes to have things written down visually (such as on a piece of paper, or mini whiteboard), to help him process the information.

Recap and rating

Share next week's topic: 'My autistic identity: Sensory'.

Before we play Lego/name activity, can you tell me:

- What did you like about the session?

- What did you learn?

- What would make it better?

If appropriate, discuss questions above and explain when you will have the next session.

Engage in the positive activity together to complete the session.

calendar

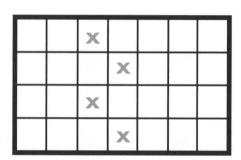

SESSION 4
My autistic identity: Sensory

Visual schedule:

1. Check in
2. Our senses
   a. Olfactory (smell)
   b. Auditory (sound)
   c. Visual (sight)
   d. Gustatory (taste)
   e. Tactile (touch)
    f. Proprioception (body awareness)
   g. Vestibular (balance)
   h. Interoception (internal body)
3. My sensory profile
4. Recap and rating
5. Positive activity, e.g., Lego
6. Back to class/home activity

Our Plan:

1. Check in
2. Our sense
   → olfactory (smell)
   → auditory (sound)
   → visual (sight)
   → gustatory (taste)
   → tactile (touch)
   → proprioception (body awareness)
   → vestibular (balance)
   → interoception (internal body)
3. My sensory profile
4. Recap and rating
5. Lego
6. Back to class/ lunch

Key messages

- We take in information through our senses, it goes to our brain to be processed, and then tells our body whether we want to do anything.

- We can be over-reactive, under-reactive or have fluctuating reactivity.

- It is important to be aware of your own sensory needs, and to ask for adaptations for these from others.

DOI: 10.4324/9781003350743-13

Resources

- Fidget tools.

- Mini-whiteboard or paper for sensory sketch.

- If the young person would benefit from seeing examples visually, write out the examples from Chapter 4 of this guidebook. You can cut them up onto different pieces of paper and make it into a sorting activity or have it as a checklist for them to highlight ones they feel are relevant. Try to tailor the explanation/examples you give to match the young person. Include examples teachers/parents/carers have shared.

Common questions/comments

Sometimes I can be fine with a certain noise/smell/fabric etc. and other times I'm not...	Your sensory processing can fluctuate (change) based on different sensory input, but also how you are feeling. So, if you are ill, anxious or tired, you may be more sensitive to certain input than at other times.
People tell me to stop doing things like tapping my pencil, but I can't stop!	People sometimes say things like that because it can be distracting for others, and they don't understand why you are doing it. You could say something like 'it helps me to concentrate – can you think of something else I can do that is less distracting?' Or try to think of some alternative plans for different situations. Remember, your sensory need will still be there, so if there is a genuine reason why you need to stop it, you will need to do something else to replace it.

Possible prompts
Check in

- Use a visual emotion check-in tool here, such as the basic EmEn Check-in (which we will cover in more detail later in the book) so the young person can share how they are feeling.

- Recap the last session (social and communication).

You may want to refer back to the 'Autistic identity traits guidance' section from Session 2 before you start this section.

Sensory sensitivity

- For this section, I recommend drawing it (on a piece of paper or mini-whiteboard) while you are going through each stage.

- You can start with a simple line across the page, and then add each section as you cover it, so you end up with something like this:

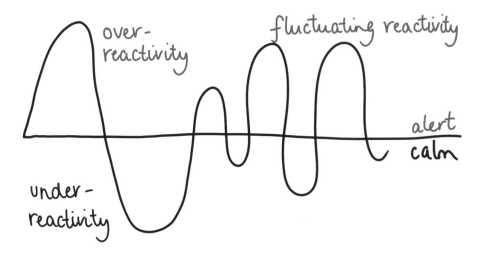

- As you go through the different types of reactivity, ask the young person if they can think of times when they've felt like this.

Here are some prompts for each of the sensory traits

**Olfactory****(Smell)**	• Some autistic people are very sensitive to smells. • If you are under-reactive to smells, you may enjoy certain smells and find them comforting. • Alternatively, if you are over-reactive, there may be certain smells that you hate, or you may find it difficult if there are strong smells, like perfume. Additional prompts: • May love certain smells or dislike particular smells. • May sniff people, objects, or food to assess the situation or gain pleasure (e.g., may be able to identify who the lost jumper belongs to by smelling it). • Holds nose to avoid certain smells. • 'Seeing smells' or combining several of the senses, is known as synaesthesia – you may want to explore this further together via resources shared on national websites.

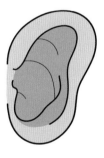**Auditory****(Sound)**	• Some autistic people are very sensitive to sounds. • These are usually sounds that are out of our control and unpredictable, such as emergency service vehicles, phones ringing, thunder or announcements at stations. • They can also be quieter sounds such as buzzing from electrical devices, scratching or tapping. • Other people (usually neurotypical) might not even notice the sounds you are aware of. • If you are over-reactive to sounds, you might experience these sounds more intensely than others and things like ear-defenders can be useful.

(Continued)

	• If you are under-reactive, you might seek louder sounds than others, or create them yourself by banging and tapping things. • Remember, you can be a mixture of the two (fluctuating-reactivity). Additional prompts: • Sensitive to certain sounds - covers ears. • Prefers to wear ear defenders/ear plugs. • Hums or sings to block out noises. • Puts ear close to noises to listen. • Enjoys the same sounds on repeat. • Difficulties knowing where a sound is coming from. • Hard to do work if there's any background noise.

 **Visual (Sight)**	• Some autistic people can be over-reactive to visual input (through their eyes) and may not like things like bright lights or walls with lots of things stuck up on them. • You may be able to pick up on tiny visual details that other people miss. • If you are under-reactive with this sense, you may not see as much detail, and need to touch things to recognise them. You may enjoy bright colours and reflections or enjoy moving things in front of your eyes. • Remember, again, you can be a combination of the two – fluctuating-reactivity. Additional prompts: • Ability to focus on small details. • Flicking fingers in front of eyes. • Liking to turn lights on and off. • Enjoying the visual movement of sprinkling, throwing, lining up or dropping objects. • Liking the environment to look a certain way, e.g., drawers all closed, doors closed, curtains just so and objects lined up or placed exactly in the correct position.

**Gustatory** **(Taste)**	• Some autistic people are over-reactive to certain tastes. Some foods can taste too strong, and you may not be able to eat them, even if you are really hungry. • Some people have such a strong sense of taste that they can tell what shop the item is bought from, or if it's a different brand. • If you are over-reactive, you may have a small group of foods that you are comfortable with and might like certain foods together, or not like them to touch. • Some autistic people can be under-reactive to tastes. You may put lots of different things in your mouth or mix different flavours such as sweet and sour foods. Additional prompts: • Described as a 'fussy eater'. • Will only eat certain flavours, colours or textures such as 'beige foods/carbs' (like chips, crackers and bread). • Finds it challenging to try new foods. • Spots small changes in recipes or when someone has tried to hide an ingredient (like vegetables) in something. • May notice the change in taste if items are stored in plastic containers.

**Tactile** **(Touch)**	• Some autistic people are over-reactive to touch. It may be uncomfortable or even painful to be touched by other people, so you might avoid hugs. • Some people who are over-reactive don't like getting messy, so things like art or swimming can be difficult. • Some people are under-reactive to touch. • You may have an injury that you don't notice. • You may like pressure, tight clothes and heavy objects, enjoying rough play. • Sometimes people say 'you don't know your own strength' as you hug others tightly. • You may chew on your sleeves or put things in your mouth. • You may like to touch things to keep you focused.

(Continued)

	Additional prompts:
	<ul><li>Likes firm massage/squeezing/hugs (deep pressure).</li><li>Very sensitive to touch - may avoid hugs and close contact.</li><li>Avoids bare feet.</li><li>May put objects in the mouth.</li><li>Chews on sleeves or collars.</li><li>Avoids gluing, painting, and sand play.</li><li>Always seeking to touch things.</li><li>Loves messy activities.</li><li>Does not notice if food is in the mouth after eating.</li></ul>

The following three are examples of sensitivity in this area:

 **Irritating clothing**	<ul><li>Finds dressing very stressful – may avoid certain textures.</li><li>Cuts out labels and tags – may feel itchy.</li><li>Doesn't like sensation of wearing shoes and socks – might find the seams irritating or hard to line them up so that they feel 'right'.</li><li>Prefers old clothing or comfier garments.</li></ul>

 **Brushing teeth**	<ul><li>Finds this overwhelming – the taste of the toothpaste and it touching the teeth and gums.</li></ul>

Having a haircut

- Finds these sensations overwhelming:
  - The hairdresser/barber standing so close.
  - The hairdresser/barber touching me.
  - The cutting of my hair.
  - The hair dropping down onto me.
  - The buzzing of clippers or razors.

Proprioception (Body awareness)

- Your proprioceptive sense is what tells you where you are in the space around you.
- If you close your eyes (or you close your eyes and demonstrate) can you tell me how you are sitting? Where are your hands? Where are your legs/feet?
- Our proprioceptive sense is what helps us know how much force to use, so we don't knock things over.
- It helps us to do up our top button, tie an apron behind our back, brush the hair at the back of our head (where we can't see) and do up the clasp on a necklace without looking.
- Differences with proprioception may mean you get described as 'clumsy' because you spill things or knock things over.
- You may press down really hard when you write or find handwriting difficult. You may bump into things or walk with a stomp/heavy footed.

(Continued)

	Additional prompts:
	• Often spills a drink because uses the wrong amount of force.
	• Writes really hard so that marks go through to the other side.
	• Described as clumsy.
	• Described as heavy footed.
	• Described as heavy handed.
	• Difficulties with fine and gross motor skills (handwriting?).
	• Bumps into things.

 **Vestibular (Balance)**	• Your vestibular sense is your sense of balance and is closely linked to the eyes and ears. Stand up and try and balance on one leg. OK, now try closing your eyes… Identify that this is harder without the sense of sight involved.
	• Your vestibular sense keeps you upright when standing on a train or bending down to pick something up. If you jump into a swimming pool and are underwater, it's what tells you which way the surface is.
	• If you are under-reactive with your vestibular sense, you may really enjoy rocking and spinning, and are able to do these without getting dizzy. You may love things that make you feel out of balance, like roller coasters or balancing at the top of a climbing frame.
	• If you are over-reactive, you might find it difficult changing directions when running, or walking on uneven surfaces. As this links with your eyes/visual sense, this can be harder if you are walking across a highly patterned carpet, for example. Balancing may be more difficult, and you may feel really dizzy after spinning, jumping or a car journey.

(Continued)

	Additional prompts:
	• Enjoys the sensation of rocking back and forth. • Enjoys spinning – can be indulged in without getting dizzy. • Seeks out experiences that challenge the feeling of stability and balance, e.g., roller coasters. • Craves 'risky' sensations – balancing on thin supports or climbing to the top of precarious heights. • Is slower at changing direction of movement when running. • Finds it difficult to maintain speed. • Finds it trickier walking and balancing. • Avoids experiences that accentuate feelings of dizziness, e.g., balancing or roller coasters. • Finds it difficult to sit up straight at a desk. • Sits in a 'W' shape (knees in front, ankles and feet to the side). • Can avoid moving the head when bending over. • May get motion sick in the car. • Avoids movement-based activities such as PE, sports or other such tasks and prefers sedentary activities. • Gets dizzy easily.

| 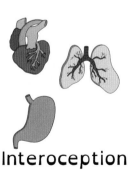
Interoception
(Internal body
sense) | • Interoception is the sense inside your body that tells you what's going on inside.
• Differences with processing in this area may mean you struggle to identify:
  ◦ If you need the toilet.
  ◦ If you are hungry or are full up.
  ◦ If you are hot or cold.
  ◦ If you are thirsty.
  ◦ If you are unwell.
  ◦ If you are itchy.
  ◦ The physical sensations of emotions, e.g., heart beating fast because you're feeling anxious.
• Feelings of being hot or cold may seem to be different from others - your teacher may tell you to take your coat off as it's a hot day, but it doesn't feel hot to you. |

My sensory profile

For each one, we can go back over your answers and write in the things that you like and don't like, and ideas of strategies that might help you.

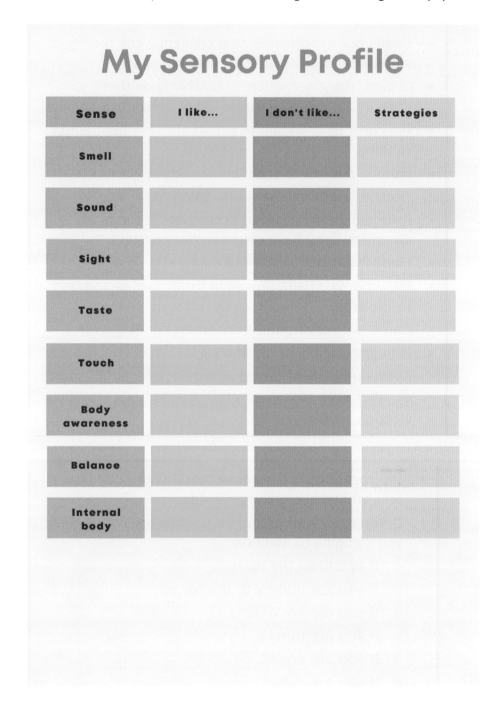

Sense	I like...	I don't like...	Strategies
Smell			
Sound			
Sight			
Taste			
Touch			
Body awareness			
Balance			
Internal body			

Here are some examples of strategies (note, some activities can be both calming and alerting):

Sense	Over-reactivity	Under-reactivity
Olfactory (smell)	• Use unscented products and unflavoured toothpaste. • Avoid perfume and share preferences with others close to you.	• Use scented lotions between activities. • Spray citrus room spray before doing work. • Use scented materials in projects.
Auditory (sound)	• Ear defenders/ear plugs. • Work in quiet environment. • Consider music with soft, even beat.	• Use sound producing resources. • Consider music with varied pitch or beat.
Visual (sight)	• Low lighting. • Workstation. • Pastel coloured paper.	• Bright lighting. • Use a highlighter to underline text. • Brightly coloured paper. • Work on a slant board.
Gustatory (taste)	• Drink from sports bottle. • Chew/suck on a sensory keychain or necklace. • Take small bites. • Blow whistles, bubbles etc.	• Eat crunchy foods such as carrots. • Eat chewy foods. • Eat ice or ice lollies. • Have a water bottle with cold water in at your desk.

(Continued)

(Continued)

Sense	Over-reactivity	Under-reactivity
Tactile (touch)	• Try a weighted blanket. • Use resistive putty. • Find materials that are calming to you, e.g., fur, velvet etc. Attach these to your book, under the desk or in your pocket.	• Consider tight clothes underneath your outfit. • Weighted blanket. • Hold something cool. • Gently and quickly rub the skin. • Wash your face with cold water. • Use a fidget tool. • Stroke an animal or soft toy.
Proprioception (body awareness)	• Request to stand at start/end of line when lining up. • Sit on chair instead of on the floor. • Push heavy furniture (request 'heavy jobs' such as carrying books). • Try a weighted blanket. • Wear a backpack or bumbag.	• Move furniture to edges of room to make it easier to move around. • Put coloured tape on the floor/desk to show boundaries. • Exercise, dance, wiggle. • Request movement-based tasks. • Try 'arm's length rule' when considering how close to stand.
Vestibular (balance)	• Take a break and do an 'errand'. • Request 'heavy jobs' such as carrying books or laundry between tasks. • Rock in rocking chair or swing. • Request visual cues for stops in movement activities.	• Jump on trampoline or do jumping jacks. • Hang upside down on climbing frame. • Ride a scooter. • Bounce on a yoga ball. • Bend over and put head between your legs. • Stand and spin round. • Request 'heavy jobs' such as carrying books or laundry between tasks.

(Continued)

(Continued)

Sense	Over-reactivity	Under-reactivity
Interoception (internal body)	• Try yoga/meditation to increase awareness of body parts and how they are feeling. • Try breathing exercises to feel calmer and be able to focus on small signs about what is going on inside the body (look up 'figure of 8 breathing' and 'box breathing'). • Try 'alerting' activities that get you out of breath, to get to know what a racing heart feels like (link this to emotions). • Look in the mirror and get to know what your body and face looks like for your own feelings and emotions.	

Reiterate that your young person may want to share these insights with school/ home to help others understand their preferences.

Recap and rating

Share next week's topic: 'Stimming, routines, masking and emotions'.

Before we play Lego/name activity, can you tell me:

- What did you like about the session?
- What did you learn?
- What would make it better?

If appropriate, discuss the questions above and explain when you will have the next session.

calendar

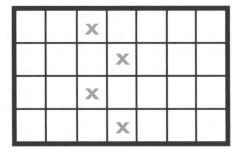

Engage in the positive activity together to complete the session.

SESSION 5

My autistic identity: Routine and structure
My autistic identity: Masking, stimming
My autistic identity: Emotions and energy levels

Visual schedule:

1. Check in
2. Stimming
3. Routine and structure
4. Masking
5. Emotions and energy levels
6. Recap and rating
7. Positive activity e.g., Lego
8. Back to class/home activity

Our Plan:

1. Check in
2. Stimming
3. Routine and structure
4. masking
5. Emotions + energy levels
6. Recap and rating
7. Lego
8. Back to class / lunch

Key messages

- Stimming can be a way of expressing joy, as well as a coping strategy.

- You shouldn't be made to feel that stimming is wrong.

- Routines may be important to make you feel calm and prepared.

- Masking describes times when you behave in a certain way to fit in with others.

- You shouldn't do things just to please other people, as in the long term, this will make you feel tired and sad.

DOI: 10.4324/9781003350743-14

- It can be useful to check in with your emotions and energy levels each day.

- There may be things you can do to change these.

- It can be hard to know how you are feeling – this links with your internal body awareness sense (interoception).

Resources

- Fidget tools.

- Mini-whiteboard or paper for drawings to support explanations.

Common questions/comments

When I stim at home/school, people always tell me to stop…	Unfortunately, people don't always understand the purpose of the stim because it isn't something they do. You shouldn't be made to feel that you are doing something wrong. It may help to explain the purpose of the stim for you – perhaps it makes you feel calmer, or it's a way of expressing your emotions.
I don't like routines – I prefer things to be a surprise.	Think back to the autism constellation and colour wheel. We are all different. Each autistic person is different. You won't have exactly the same traits as another person, which is why we are personalising this book, so it is just about you.
I have to mask so people like me.	Making friends is really hard. But long term, behaving in a way that isn't authentic to your true self won't make you happy. There are times when we do certain things to be polite, or to follow rules, but you should always stay true to your identity. If you are struggling to find friends, see if your school can set up an interest club or if you can find a local autistic social group or forum online.

Possible prompts
Check in

- Use a visual emotion check-in tool here, such as the basic EmEn Check-in (which we will cover in more detail later in the book) so the young person can share how they are feeling.

- Recap the last session (sensory).

You may want to refer back to the 'Autistic identity traits guidance' section from Session 2 before you start this section.

Stimming

- Explore examples of times when the young person may stim. Add their comments to the box next to the picture.

- Can they think of a time when they were told to stop stimming? Discuss this and reinforce the fact that it is a personal choice to stim.

Stimming

Routine and structure

Knowing the plan

- Some autistic people like to know what the plan is. They may like to know the schedule in school, what's expected in the lesson, or what they are doing at the weekend.

- Can you think of routines that are important to you? How do you feel when things change without any warning?

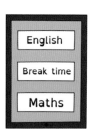

Knowing the plan

Time to recharge/recover

- Some autistic people find they can feel really worn out, or drained. This might be especially so after lots of social interaction, times when a plan has changed, unpleasant sensory experiences or if things feel out of control.

Time to recharge/ recover

Things I do to help me feel calm and prepared

Things I do to help me feel calm and prepared:

- What things help you to feel calm and prepared?

- Try to give examples specific to them, for example:

  ○ Do they like to have a laminated timetable in their pocket so they remember what lesson to go to?

  ○ Do they keep their books in colour-coded plastic wallets, so they know what subject they are for?

Masking

- Go through the effects of masking.

- This may be more common in girls (but occurs for girls and boys). It can look like 'copying' behaviour which is analytical rather than intuitive. Observation powers can be a strength!

- Young people may have been described as being 'fine' in school due to this.

- Explore any of these further if they are unsure of the meanings.

- Add their own examples to the box.

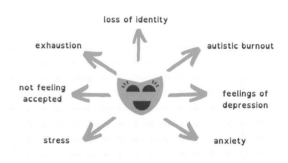

the effects of masking

Masking

What would help me to be my true autistic self?

- Prompt the young person to think of things that would help them to be their true autistic self and mask less.

- Examples may include:

  ○ Sharing their autistic identity with others.

  ○ Asking for time and space.

  ○ Finding out more about other autistic individuals, so they feel represented and have possible role models.

Energy levels

- Discuss other examples when our energy levels may not match the energy level needed for the activity. For example:

  ○ Sports activities when you need lots of energy but are feeling tired.

  ○ When you want to relax but you are 'buzzing'.

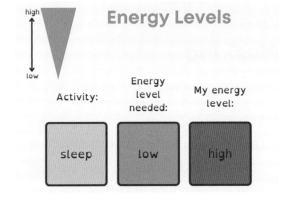

  ○ Going to a party but you don't have the energy for socialising.

Emotions

- This section includes three different types of visual emotional check-in tool, that vary in complexity:

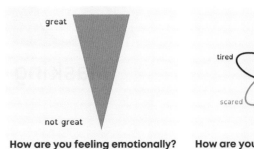

1. Great/not great.

2. Six emotions words (with optional 1–5 scaling).

3. More detailed emotion Venn diagram.

Consider your young person and which one you think is most appropriate for them, based on the emotional vocabulary and understanding they already have. You may want to go through all three, as they build on one another, or just refer to one of them if you feel they could be overwhelming. If they do not currently have a visual check-in tool for their emotions, it would be useful to choose one of these to embed into their future routine. The EmEn Check-in is available from the downloads section online, but if you want the young person to choose from the six emotions words, and scale where they are for this emotion, you do not have to have a set template – a mini-whiteboard or piece of paper will do just fine.

Remember, our understanding of emotions is a life-long task! This is just a starting point, to give some visual tools to support identification and communication of emotions. The more these tools are used, and the young person's understanding of emotions is explored, the more this will become embedded in their vocabulary.

To recap on the potential difficulties around understanding emotions, refer back to Chapter 5 earlier in the book.

Exploring the emotions further

After you have looked at the physical responses for feeling angry, you may want to explore each of the six emotions in the same way, looking at the physical responses to each. Your young person may find it difficult to identify how they feel, so you could:

- Watch videos related to each emotion.

- Keep an emotion diary/book with colour-coded pages related to each emotion, where you can add examples.

- Explore emotions in book characters, films, TV and within your family/classmates.

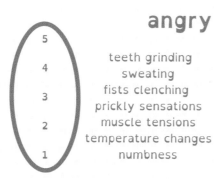

angry

teeth grinding
sweating
fists clenching
prickly sensations
muscle tensions
temperature changes
numbness

Physical response

- Model emotions regularly out loud, e.g., "My heart is beating quite fast and I'm about to have a meeting. I think I'm feeling a bit scared."

- Over time expand this to include possible responses, e.g., "I'm going to take some deep breaths and watch a two-minute funny video to try and calm me down."

If looking at the emotion Venn diagram, check if there are any that the young person doesn't know. Look them up together and consider creating an emotion book to explore this further.

Here you can work through as many emotions as you feel appropriate at this time (but beware of overwhelming them!). You may want to do a few and then come back to it at another time.

My EmEn Check-in

- This is a check-in tool that combines your energy levels and emotions.

- The young person can look at what they need to do today (or their schedule), and how they are feeling. This can help to give them a plan for what to do to be ready for their day, or the thing they are about to do. This might be different each day, so it can be useful to check in each morning.

- Try to be realistic – you might want to sleep all day, but if you've got an exam, that's probably not really an option!

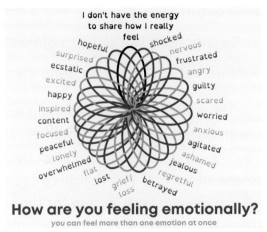

How are you feeling emotionally?
you can feel more than one emotion at once

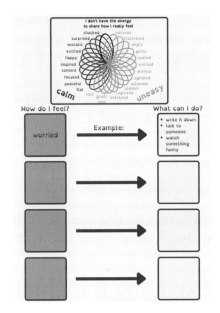

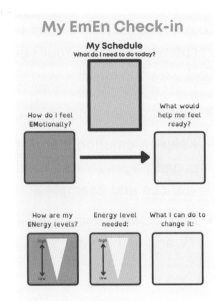

Anxiety

- This could be an insightful exercise to see what is important to the young person.

- If they feel any are relevant to them, explore them together and try to come up with a plan of action.

- For example, if they don't have enough time with their interests and other people, could there be an opportunity at lunchtime for them to spend time researching their passion, with a carefully selected peer (sitting outside the staff room, or in the office so there is no additional adult supervision required)?

Feelings of anxiety

My autistic identity summary

- You may want to refer to the contents page to show they have completed the section exploring 'My autistic identity'.

Recap and rating

Share next week's topic: 'Other autistic individuals, your toolkit and personal passport and self-advocacy'.

Remind the young person that this will be the final section of the book.

Before we play Lego/name activity, can you tell me:

- What did you like about the session?

- What did you learn?

- What would make it better?

If appropriate, discuss questions above and explain when you will have the next session.

Engage in the positive activity together to complete the session.

SESSION 6

Other autistic individuals
My toolkit
My personal passport
My autistic identity statement
Self-advocacy

Visual schedule:

1. Check in
2. Other autistic individuals
3. My toolkit
4. My personal passport
5. My autistic identity statement
6. Self-advocacy
7. Summary
8. Recap and rating
9. Positive activity, e.g., Lego
10. Back to class/home activity

Our Plan:

1. Check in
2. Other autistic individuals
3. My toolkit
4. My personal passport
5. My autism identity statement
6. Self-advocacy
7. Summary
8. Recap and rating
9. Lego
10. Back to class/lunch

Note: this section has a lot of reflective content. Depending on the young person you are working with, they may want to spend longer on each activity, or come back to some tasks after additional reflection time.

Key messages

- There are lots of other autistic individuals in the world.
- I will share traits with these individuals (think back to the colour wheel), but we are not the same.
- My toolkit, autism statement and passport are all tools to help me self-advocate.
- Self-advocacy is when you tell people your thoughts and feelings and ask for what you need.

DOI: 10.4324/9781003350743-15

Resources

- Fidget tools.

Common questions/comments

I don't like any of the same things as the other autistic people.	Remember, everyone's different. There are many autistic people. We can look up other autistic individuals and see if we can find anyone who shares your interests.
I don't want anyone else to know that I'm autistic.	Your identity is personal to you. It is up to you who you want to share your autistic identity with. There are some benefits to sharing: others may understand you better, you may be more likely to get any support that you need, sharing may make you feel more proud of your autistic identity, you may be more likely to meet others who share this identity and you might inspire others to feel proud of their own autistic identity. You can choose to share if and when you are ready.

Possible prompts
Check in

- Use a visual emotion check-in tool here, such as the basic EmEn Check-in so the young person can share how they are feeling.

- Recap the last session (stimming, routines, masking and emotions).

Other autistic individuals

- Explore the profiles shared.

- You can also tailor this to the young person and research other autistic individuals who may share their interests or passions.

- More and more people are sharing their autistic identities, so an internet search will give you access to other well-known individuals.

My toolkit

- Explore the tips in the workbook – are there any they think may be useful?

- Support the young person to add their own strategies to their toolkit.

- Give plenty of processing time – this could be something you keep coming back to.

My personal passport

- Ask the young person if they would like support completing this and then go through each section.

- Support the young person to be specific.
  Ideas could include:

  - Slow down when you talk.

  - Ask me one thing at a time.

  - Don't stand too close to me.

  - Talk quietly.

  - Give me a fidget tool etc.

My autism identity statement

- This gives the young person a template or 'set phrase' to use if someone asks them what autism means.

- Support the young person to complete the sentences.

Self-advocacy

- Double empathy problem: why do they think it's called this? Look at the diagram and explore the fact that it works both ways – it can be difficult for people to understand each other.

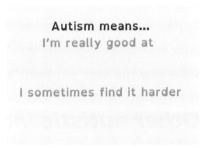

Autism means...
I'm really good at

I sometimes find it harder

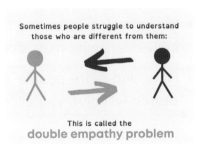

Sometimes people struggle to understand those who are different from them:

This is called the
double empathy problem

Telling others

- Have they told anyone already? Discuss.

- Is there anything that worries them about telling people? Explore these and plan for possible eventualities.

- We can never control what other people say or do, but if we are proud of who we are, we don't let it affect our autistic pride!

Recap and rating

Before we play Lego/name activity, can you tell me:

- What did you like about the session?

- What did you learn?

- What would make it better?

Engage in the positive activity together to complete the session.

The end of the book

- Celebrate the time you have spent together.

- Reflect on their learning overall.

- Consider if they would like to share this book with anyone else (perhaps show someone at school/home).

- Think about how they will use this book in the future. The contents page means they can dip in and out of the book if they want to think about a particular area.

- They may want to develop their own ongoing workbooks. Consider buying personalised notebooks or encourage them to set up their own system to help process information on an ongoing basis. This could be recording voice notes, videos or typing into a document.

- Reinforce that our understanding of our identity is a life-long journey. Encourage them to keep finding out more about autism (you could explore YouTubers, or social media accounts, depending on their age).

RESOURCES

Information gathering (to be completed in an informal meeting with parents/carers or other key adults who know the young person):

Area	Comments from parents/carers/key adults
Understanding of autism e.g., has this been discussed previously? What words have been used?	
Session planning e.g., times of day/lessons to avoid, rooms to avoid, things that would help create a positive atmosphere/activity to end session	
Likes/dislikes e.g., food, activities, lessons, programmes, music, sports etc.	
Personality traits e.g., calm, friendly, serious, honest, talkative etc.	
Interests and focus e.g., being able to focus all attention on one topic/activity, imagination, interests, switching attention, organisation etc.	

(Continued)

DOI: 10.4324/9781003350743-16

(Continued)

Area	Comments from parents/carers/ key adults
Social and communication e.g., talking to new people, working in groups/alone, busy places, processing verbal input, playing with others, communication preferences, echolalia, ways of showing they care etc.	
Sensory e.g., taste, touch, smell, sound, sight, proprioception, vestibular, interoception etc.	
Stimming e.g., as a calming activity or expression of emotion.	
Routine and structure e.g., knowing the plan, coping with change, time to recharge, things that they find calming etc.	
Masking e.g., examples of situations in which they mask, things that help them be their true self.	
Emotions and energy levels e.g., understanding of emotions and ability to communicate and respond to them.	

Red/green cards

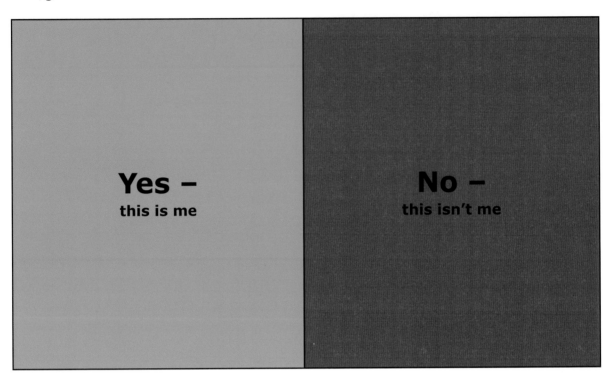

For more strategies, information
and resources, visit:

rebeccaduffus.com

@rebeccaduffus
@rebecca.duffus

REFERENCES

Gaigg, S. B., Crawford, S., & Cottell, H. (2019). *An evidence-based guide to anxiety in autism* [online]. Available at: www.city.ac.uk/__data/assets/pdf_file/0010/466039/Anxiety-in-Autism-A5-guide.pdf (Accessed: 18 May 2022).

Kenny, L., Hattersley, C., Molins, B., Buckley, C., Povey, C., & Pellicano, E. (2016). Which terms should be used to describe autism? Perspectives from the UK autism community. *Autism*, 20(4): 442–462.

Lai, M. C., Lombardo, M. V., Auyeung, B., Chakrabarti, B., & Baron-Cohen, S. (2015). Sex/gender differences and autism: Setting the scene for future research. *Journal of the American Academy of Child and Adolescent Psychiatry*, 54(1): 11–24.

Loomes, R., Hull, L., & Mandy, W. P. L. (2017). What is the male-to-female ratio in autism spectrum disorder? A systematic review and meta-analysis. *Journal of the American Academy of Child and Adolescent Psychiatry*, 56(6): 466–474.

Marco, E. J., Hinkley, L. B., Hill, S. S., & Nagarajan, S. S. (2011). Sensory processing in autism: A review of neurophysiologic findings. *Pediatric Research*, 69(5 Pt 2): 48R–54R.

Murray, D. K. C. (1992). 'Attention Tunnelling and Autism', in *Living with autism: The individual, the family, and the professional.* Originally presented at the Durham Conference, UK. Proceedings obtainable from Autism Research Unit, School of Health Sciences, University of Sunderland, Sunderland SR2 7EE, UK.

Purkis, Y. (2017). *Yenn Purkis: Thoughts on all things autism and mental health* [online]. Available at: https://yennski.com/2017/04/09/why-we-need-to-say-goodbye-to-functioning-labels/ (Accessed: 11 April 2022).

Sainsbury, C. (2010). *Martian in the playground: Understanding the schoolchild with Asperger's syndrome*. Thousand Oaks, CA: Sage.

van Steensel, F. J., Bögels, S. M., & Perrin, S. (2011). Anxiety disorders in children and adolescents with autistic spectrum disorders: A meta-analysis. *Clinical Child and Family Psychology Review*, 14(3): 302–317.

INDEX